LIVING
in a
STEP-
FAMILY
without Getting
STEPPED ON

For more information about seminars or speaking engagements with Dr. Kevin Leman, please write to him at:

P.O. Box 35370
Tucson, AZ 85740

If you prefer, you may call Dr. Leman at (520) 797-3830 or send him a fax at (520) 797-3809.

To become a realFAMILIES club member, call toll-free (877) 4 REAL US.

Web site: realfamilies.com

LIVING in a STEP-FAMILY without Getting STEPPED On

DR. KEVIN LEMAN

A JANET THOMA BOOK

THOMAS NELSON PUBLISHERS
Nashville

This book is affectionately dedicated to my mom, May Leman, for always loving me.

Published in Nashville, Tennessee, by Thomas Nelson, Inc.

Library of Congress Cataloging-in-Publication Data

Leman, Kevin.
    Living in a stepfamily without getting stepped on / Kevin Leman.
      p. cm.
    ISBN 0-7852-6601-1 (pb)
    ISBN 0-8407-3492-1 (hc)
    1. Stepfamilies.   2. Title.
HQ759.92.L45 1994
306.874—dc20   94-3565
                                    CIP

Printed in the United States of America
2 3 4 5 6 — 05 04 03 02 01

CONTENTS

PART ONE

Why Stepfamilies Face the Birth Order Blender

CHAPTER 1

They Thought They Would Live Happily Blended Ever After, and Then . . .

Phil C., a regional sales manager for a large computer firm, looked the part: early forties, clean-cut, wearing the carefully pressed custom suit, the fine silk tie, the Gucci shoes. He had invited me to lunch, explaining that he had heard me speak at a conference a few weeks earlier and that he was interested in my "availability for other engagements." Since it sounded like a good contact—I speak for many corporations, companies, and organizations—I accepted. Besides, he was buying.

But as Phil and I chatted, I could tell he had something else in mind besides my speaking for a group of sales reps at some posh resort.

"You know, Dr. Leman, when Peggy—that's my wife—and I decided to attend your birth order session at that conference in Chicago last month, we didn't know what to expect. But after the first few minutes, we were chuckling and elbowing each other. It was as if you had been looking in our windows or reading our mail. You had her kids and my kids nailed to a tee, describing what happens on a daily basis in our home. It was almost uncanny."

"Well, sometimes I can get lucky. Birth order doesn't always fit everyone perfectly," I told him, "but it is amazing how often it does connect."

"Well, you sure connected with us. My firstborn son, Lance, is a classic example of the conscientious, hard-driving type. And Peggy's firstborn daughter, Carol, is Miss Perfectionist Plus. Peggy's got a middle child, Patrick, who's gone just the other direction from Carol. He's the family jock—a terrific volleyball player—and couldn't care less about school. And oh, yes, Peggy's last born, Tina, is definitely the charming entertainer—she keeps us all in stitches."

"The typical characteristics of birth order often fit kids to a tee," I commented. "Come to think of it, Phil, I think I can guess your birth order. I've already gotten some pretty good hints."

"Well, sure, I guess so," he allowed, "but I don't know how you could tell so soon. This is the first time we've met, and we've only been talking for about thirty-five minutes."

"Well, the expensive suit, the very fashionable tie, and the alligator shoes all point in one basic direction. But maybe what really clinches it is your digital watch. I would say you're the firstborn male of your family."

"Guilty!" laughed Phil. "I'm the oldest in my family, and I have a younger sister and two other brothers. But how can you tell just from looking at what I'm wearing?

A lot of sales managers wear suits and ties. And everybody wears a watch."

"Yes, but your suit is perfectly pressed. Your tie has no signs of having been to lunch in other restaurants, and your shoes gleam like diamonds. In other words, you're what I call impeccably groomed, and this is always a big tip-off on firstborns. It's true, of course, that other birth orders may dress impeccably, too, but there is just something about the way you carry yourself and the way you talk that led me down the firstborn lane."

"Okay, but what's this about my watch?"

"Note that it's *digital*—capable of giving you the exact time, not to mention the date and several other functions, all of which point to a certain amount of perfectionism, another telltale trait of the firstborn. But I don't really think you invited me to lunch to guess your birth order or even to talk about speaking for another company conference some time. I heard you mention 'her' kids and 'my' kids. I hope I'm not making too personal an observation, but you're in a blended family, right?"

"Yes, and you're not getting too personal at all. In fact, I hope you don't mind if I tell you about my family because I guess that's really why I'm here. I've been remarried for about two years. Peggy and I both came out of lousy marriages—at the end there was no communication, no trust, no working together, and almost nonexistent sex."

"How did you and Peggy meet?" I asked.

"Through some mutual friends. My life was transformed in a matter of weeks. Everything seemed to fall into place, and even our kids all seemed in favor of us getting married. We made them part of the wedding, and we thought we were going to live happily ever after in one big blended family—my two, her three, and us, almost a Brady Bunch—and if you include the golden retriever my kids and I brought along, we do have the Brady Bunch numbers."

"But you're here to tell me that the Brady Bunch you're not," I said.

"I'd say it's more like 'Married With Children.' As I said, her kids and mine both acted like they really wanted us to get married, but when we came home from our honeymoon, the tension started almost immediately. When I show any interest in Peggy's girls, in particular, my second born, Tiffany, really gives me a bad time, anything from giving me the cold shoulder to throwing a small fit. And Peggy tells me that being stepmother to my two kids has not been much fun. She hadn't been in the house three weeks when they decided she was the wicked stepmother. We're both totally baffled because Peggy has bent over backwards to be good to my kids and give them things their mother never even tried to give them."

"Does their natural mother see them much?" I asked.

"She ran off with my supposed best friend. Seldom contacts the kids at all. But what I want to know, Dr. Leman, is where did Peggy and I go wrong? We had long talks, and we knew there would be some problems. We even got some counseling before the wedding. We thought we were ready. Everything looked so good, but now we have to admit that we weren't at all prepared for what we got into."

"Actually, I wouldn't think of it as what you did wrong, Phil. When you remarried you stepped into some typical problems that I hear about all the time. It's interesting that even though you got counseling and you thought you were ready, now you can see that you weren't prepared—that's also a situation I hear about a lot. If it's any comfort, you're like a lot of intelligent people who try to go into building a blended family with their eyes open. They somehow still buy into the myths that make them think, *Our blended family will be different.*"

"Myths? What myths?" Phil asked.

"Well, for one thing, while you admitted that you might have a few problems, you probably believed that everything would just come together and you'd have a happy, 'normal' life."

"I have to admit you're right," said Phil. "It seemed to me that we had so much going for us. The wedding went so well we thought managing our new family was going to be a piece of cake—no pun intended."

"I'm afraid you may have been indulging yourselves in a bit of denial. Not too long ago I was talking with a stepmom who said, 'Denial is so much a part of a second marriage. You want to pretend you're like everyone else, and you're not.' She's absolutely right."

Phil didn't say anything, choosing to work on his lunch and ponder what I had said. I hoped that I hadn't discouraged him, but I had wanted to make him think.

In Blended Families, E − R = D

Under the best of conditions, blending a family is no snap. Chances are, you already know this is true because you are in a stepfamily situation. In 1992, it was estimated that one out of three Americans is a stepparent, a stepchild, a stepsibling, or some other member of a stepfamily. In addition, it was estimated that more than half of all Americans have been, are now, or eventually will be in one or more stepfamily relationships during their lives.[1]

According to the Stepfamily Association of America, about 43 percent of all marriages now are remarriages for at least one of the adults. About 65 percent of remarriages involve children from previous marriages, and thus form stepfamilies. An estimated 15 to 20 million stepfamilies existed in 1998, and it was projected that one out of every three children in the United States will live in a stepfamily before they reach age eighteen.[2]

With a few years (or even a few months) in a stepfamily under your belt, it's very likely that the assumptions and expectations you had before your remarriage have been tempered by stark reality. A woman who remarried and wound up with five children instead of her original two told me, "We went through months of premarital counseling, but it didn't prepare us for being a blended family. Until you live with someone every day, you and your children with him and his children, all together under the same roof, you don't know what you're going to cope with."

This woman's honest admission can be summed up in the following equation that my colleague, Dr. Jay Passavant, and I have often quoted on *realFAMILIES.com*, a syndicated television show for parents:

$$E - R = D$$
(Expectations minus reality equals disillusionment.)

Yet, despite the odds against them, despite the bruising and shattering experience of divorce (sometimes more than one), people remain intrepid eternal optimists who try marriage again. In America alone, it was estimated in 1994 that more than thirteen hundred new families formed every day.[3] (Those figures have surely risen, since the blended family has become the most common form of family in the twenty-first century.) Most of the men and women who decide to remarry naively expect that *this* time their marriage and family life will work because they won't make the same mistakes. This time they have found Mr. Right or Mrs. Wonderful, and they will live harmoniously blended ever after.

Unfortunately, experience usually proves them wrong. As I try to help blended families make it, I can think of another equation that applies:

$$N \times R = C$$
(Naiveté times reality equals chaos.)

The key to both equations is *reality.* One of the major reasons that expectations get dashed on the rocks of reality is "the kids." As one woman who married a father of two said, "The situation is just impossible. People go into these marriages with no idea of what is involved, and it's like falling off a cliff. There's *never* enough money to go around . . ."[4]

And she could have easily added that there is never enough time, energy, or patience to go around either. The plight of many stepfamilies reminds me of a corny old joke:

Question: *What's green and goes 100 m.p.h.?*
Answer: *A frog in a blender.*

A growing army of moms, dads, and children might wryly agree that another punch line could be "A blended family." And they ought to know. Stepfamily members often feel as if they're in a blender, turning green from getting whirled violently around and around—while they're being chopped to pieces in the process.

These days with the divorce rate hovering around 50 percent, the odds are against *any* family. Put a divorced mom and her kids in the same house with a divorced dad and his kids, and those odds get even longer, increasing to 60 percent and beyond.

For over twenty years I have been working with families like Phil's—in my office, in seminars and other classroom settings, and on radio and television. Many of these families have involved remarriages—stepmothers, stepfathers, and stepchildren. From what I have seen, I have to admit that I often ask clients who are contemplating remarriage, "Are you absolutely *sure*? When you live in a stepfamily," I tell them, "you can get stepped on."

I decided I wouldn't tell Phil the blender joke. He looked a little green around the gills anyway, and, besides, he was hoping I might have some answers for his blended family problems.

Phil's Remarriage Started Well and Then . . .

Phil finished his last bite of salmon and said, "One thing that has amazed both Peggy and me is how touchy our kids have been about the simplest things. Little things, like who gets a ride to school or who gets a little help with homework, can set off a major hassle."

"The little things will do it every time," I told him. "Another myth that a lot of remarrying couples subconsciously believe is that children from broken homes adapt easily into stepfamilies. A few kids do adapt quickly, but most don't. The basic reason is that children coming into a blended family have been hurt by a divorce or the death of a parent. They have deep wounds that are barely healed over."

"Why, then, did her kids and mine act like they

thought our getting married was such a good idea?" Phil asked me.

"At first, they could have been naive, not realizing that you'd really go ahead and do it. When you announced your wedding plans, they were probably shocked but tried to be polite. You and Peggy may not have read their signals correctly. Perhaps you heard only what you wanted to hear."

"Maybe, but everybody seemed so happy at the wedding. We had a great time," Phil persisted.

"I'm not sure why the wedding went so well. Maybe the two of you had a great time while the kids just gritted their teeth. Or maybe you were just lucky. But once you came home from the honeymoon and you all moved in together, everyone realized that this was for real. Life would never be the way it was. The grief and anger and the feelings of separation and loss that all your kids were carrying were still there, and your remarriage opened up the wounds again."

"I guess I didn't realize that everyone was carrying all that baggage," Phil mused as he took a sip of coffee. "I thought my kids had pretty well gotten over my divorce. Peggy's kids seemed pretty well adjusted, too. I can see now that I was wrong and that both Peggy and I have a lot to learn about all this."

"I don't mean to make light of your problems, Phil, but our conversation has reminded me of a little play on words that I like to use tongue in cheek with the parents of a blended family. Here, I'll scratch it out on this napkin." After busying myself with a ballpoint pen for a minute or so, I showed Phil this acrostic:

B—is for bloodshed ("Nobody's pushing *me* around!")
L—is for loneliness ("I don't fit anywhere in this family.")

E—is for eternity ("Will these hassles ever end?")

N—is for naiveté ("Why can't we live like a *normal* family?")

D—is for dumbfounded ("Why did we ever get into this?")

E—is for education ("We've got to find some answers!")

D—is for determination ("We will make this work!")

"Very clever," Phil said with a wry smile. "You don't have that printed up on little cards, do you? I particularly like the last two about getting education and being determined because that's what Peggy and I really want to do. We can see that all of this is really affecting our marriage— no time or motivation to communicate, perfunctory sex, and sniping at each other more and more, particularly about the kids. Lately, I've even wondered if we should have ever tried this blended family thing."

"Well, keep in mind that a lot of supposedly normal nuclear families could identify with this acrostic, too. Actually, the good news is that you both seem to be aware that you've got a real problem on your hands. This tells me you've at least reached stage two of the process every blended family has to go through and that you'd like to move on to stage three."

"I'm sorry," Phil said, "but I haven't heard of the stages of a blended family. What are they?"

"Some counselors say there are three stages, and I know of one who outlines seven,[5] but I have typically observed four. That little acrostic I showed you was just for fun, but it does roughly parallel the stages that every blended family seems to go through. In stage one, everybody's going around saying, 'Let's walk softly,' as they try to feel each other out on how all this is going to work. The walk softly stage might last several months or only a few weeks. For some families, it's only a few days!"

"With us, I'd say it lasted maybe two weeks, and then we started in," Phil offered.

I nodded. "That's when you got into stage two—'Why did we ever do this?' In stage two, the polite sparring is over and everyone starts landing cheap shots, throwing punches, verbal and otherwise. Or maybe they're just retreating into a shell and freezing other people out. Many remarried couples I've worked with say it takes about eighteen months to get through stages one and two. Then, if the family is still together, they can begin solving their problems and becoming truly blended."

"Well, we've been at this for almost two years, and I don't think we're moving toward solving our problems yet," Phil said sadly.

"But you're searching and wanting to move into stage three. I hear you saying you want to work this thing out."

"I don't think our kids are really that interested in working it out."

"That's not too surprising," I told him. "But I think you and Peggy would like to find a way to pull it off. And if you can pull together and present a solid front to your kids, you will eventually move into stage four—'We're going to make it.' Maybe it won't be the perfect bliss you've dreamed about, but you can all have a lot more respect and peace as you function on a more positive, healthy basis."

"Respect . . . peace . . ." Phil shook his head. "I'm not sure there'll ever be a whole lot of that. We really do love each other, and if you take all the kids out of the equation, our marriage could be heaven on earth. Unfortunately, the kids will be with us for quite a few years."

"The kids are still testing you and Peggy because they've seen your first marriages fail, and they're not sure this one's going to last either. To be truthful, they're probably trying to drive a wedge between you, but once they see that this won't work, it will actually settle them down and give them feelings of security they don't have right now."

Phil glanced at his digital watch. "Dr. Leman, I want to thank you for your time. You've given me more help over this lunch than I've found anywhere since I've been in my blended family. You know, I'm not the type who goes to psychologists, but I'm wondering if there would be a way for Peggy and me to come and see you. The company allows me to take her on several trips a year, and we'll both be in Phoenix next month. Perhaps we could run down to Tucson and spend a few hours with you. Do you have time for anything like that?"

"Not as a rule, Phil, but your story intrigues me, and because you're coming from so far out of town, I'll block out the time. I really would like to talk to you and Peggy about your problems and particularly about how birth order has an awful lot to do with the tensions you're seeing between the two of you, as well as among your kids. Why don't you go back home and talk it over with Peggy, then call me and we'll set something up? Before you leave, I'd like to get your card so I can mail you a copy of *The Birth Order Book*. It would be helpful for you both to read it before you come out to see me."

Good News! There *Is* a Tunnel— and a Light

Lunch over, Phil and I went our separate ways: I headed back for my office and an afternoon filled with appointments and some paperwork; Phil caught a cab to catch a plane headed for his home in the Midwest. But we'd see each other again, I was fairly sure of that.

I could only hope that he and Peggy would read the book I planned to send them so that they'd be ready to talk about blending all the birth orders now residing—or *colliding*—under their roof.

As a counselor, I sometimes say, "Giving people hope is my business." From what I've seen of blended families, there are few who can't use a little more of that valuable commodity. As I have worked and talked with hundreds of stepparents, I've discovered that *there is hope*. There is light at the end of the tunnel. I can promise that you can burrow through the tunnel if you are patient and accept this fact: *Blending is a process, not something that happens overnight.*

One of the great enemies of a blended family is the fact that we live in the age of instant everything. It is natural for Mom and Dad to assume that they will have "instant success" with their new marriage and the new family it creates. Sometimes they naively assume that because they love each other so much and because they have found the "right" mate "this time," marriage is going to be so much more wonderful the second time around, and the kids will gladly come along for the ride.

The truth is, however, that the term *blended family* is a misnomer. It's much more accurate to say that a stepfamily is blend*ing*. It has not become completely blend*ed*, a process which may take years—or in some cases, never takes place at all.

A glance at the various dictionary definitions will tell you that to *blend* something means mingling or combining certain components so that you achieve a measure of harmony. And that's what you're trying to do in your blending family. You want to harmonize all the various personalities while doing your best to keep conflict at a minimum and avoid discriminating against one family member or another.

It's my guess you picked up this book because you're somewhere in the blending process. Perhaps you're about to successfully blend; or maybe you've been at it only a few short weeks or months and already you've got problems. You may be in the heat of the battle, wondering why you ever thought you could pull this off. You and your spouse may be pulling farther and farther apart, arguing, for example, over who should discipline whose kids (considered by many experts to be the number one issue in the blended family).

Or perhaps you're drawing closer to your spouse in desperation, standing back to back as you fight off the various forces that seem to be closing in on your relationship from all sides. You're wondering how you can work it out, and you're willing to try anything. I believe this book can help. In fact, if you master a few of the principles and skills described in the following chapters, I guarantee that you will be much better equipped to wage the battle of blending your family and come up not only a survivor but a winner!

What Makes This Book Different?

It's a fairly safe assumption that this book isn't the first information you've read about blending families. There are dozens of books that can tell you all about how to blend a family, how to be a good stepmother, how to resolve conflicts with or among your stepchildren, how to deal with the new family at your house, and on and on. Many of these books are excellent, and I'll be recommending some of them for further reading because they make excellent points about dealing with the major issues in the blended family.

Besides disciplining the children, other major issues affecting a blended family include anger, grief, and feelings of uprootedness, separation, and loss. A basic feeling I've often heard expressed by children is: "Why can't Mommy and Daddy, who are so big and powerful, solve their problem? Why can't we live together like we did before?"

Stepfamilies must also deal with the guilt everyone brings to the blended family often due to unfinished business that was left behind in a broken home. Moms and dads feel guilty because the first marriage failed, and children often believe, *If only I had behaved better— Mommy and Daddy wouldn't have gotten divorced.*

But I haven't listed all the issues. Complicating blended family life are the divided loyalties held by children who may feel betrayed because "Dad married this new woman, but what was the matter with the wife he had before?" Add to that the mixed histories that family members bring—different traditions, different values— that must be combined into one. And let's not forget the ex-spouses, who sometimes cause the biggest problems of all!

In later chapters, I will discuss all these important issues and more. But first, let's look at what makes this book a unique resource for stepfamilies. Its special ingredient is summed up in its subtitle:

Helping Your Children Survive the Birth Order Blender

Starting a blended family involves a lot more than having Mom and Dad and all the kids move in together. You're bringing together two sets of birth orders, and birth order has a lot to do with why family members look at things so differently from one another. Call it *different personalities,* if you please, but if there is anything a blended family needs to understand, it's *who is who and why each person is the way he or she is.*

This issue could be one of the most important issues of all: When children from two different families are brought together by the marriage of their parents, all of them are plunged into the birth order blender.

Do You Know What Your Birth Order Is?

"Just what," you may ask, "is the birth order blender, and why is it such a big deal?" First, let's take a short quiz on personality traits. I will give you four different sets of characteristics, followed by the same multiple choice answers: firstborn, middle child, last born, only child. Choose one answer only for each question:

1. *If you are manipulative and charming; if you blame others and show off; if you are a people person and a good salesperson; if you are precocious and engaging, you have the characteristics of a:*
___ *A. Firstborn*   ___ *C. Last born*
___ *B. Middle child*   ___ *D. Only child*

2. *If you are perfectionistic, reliable, conscientious, list oriented, well organized, critical, serious, scholarly, you have the characteristics of a:*
___ *A. Firstborn*   ___ *C. Last born*
___ *B. Middle child*   ___ *D. Only child*

3. *If you are a mediator, an avoider of conflict, and an independent person; if you have the fewest pictures in the family photo album; if you are extremely loyal to*

the peer group, have many friends, or are a maverick, you have the characteristics of a:

___A. Firstborn   ___C. Last born
___B. Middle child   ___D. Only child

4. If you are a super achiever; if you are very "adult" in your behavior; if you can't stand failure, are extremely dependable, have very high expectations for yourself, and have always been more comfortable with people older or younger than you are, you have the characteristics of a:

___A. Firstborn   ___C. Last born
___B. Middle child   ___D. Only child

How did you do? Question 1 describes typical characteristics of last born babies of the family. Question 2 describes the firstborns. Question 3 describes middle children, those born somewhere between first and last. Question 4 describes only children, who are super firstborns and then some.

We'll be taking a much more thorough look at each of these birth orders to learn how their strengths and weaknesses blend or collide in the typical stepfamily. To give you just one brief example, suppose two firstborn children from either side of the blended family are flaw-finding perfectionists. Suppose also that in their newly blended family, they have to share the same bedroom. Need I say more?

After over twenty years of working with families involved in remarriages—stepmothers, stepfathers, and stepchildren—I am convinced that the couple who understands how to blend the birth orders of their children (not to mention their *own* birth orders) has a much better chance of survival and (with lots of prayer and hard work) success. When you become aware of the significance of each person's birth order, as well as the phenomenal power of the life-style and life theme that each person brings to the family, you will be able to avoid, or at least cope with more ably, the pitfalls of remarriage with children.

In the chapters coming up, I want to show you not only how and why birth orders collide, but also what you can do about it. At the same time, you'll be taking a brief refresher (or introductory) course on the major characteristics of each birth order. So let's get started!

NOTES

1. Statistics from the Stepfamily Association of America Web site, www.stepfam.org; accessed 2/9/01.

2. Ibid. 1998 statistic from Diocese of Cleveland, www.dioceseofcleveland.org/mfm/stepfamilies.htm; accessed 2/9/01.

3. This statistic was found on www.psychpages.com, where psychologist Dr. Debra Moore shares information on psychology and health issues. Accessed 2/13/01.

4. Barbara Hustedt Crook, "His, Heirs, Theirs—Binuclear Family Ties," *Cosmopolitan*, August 1991, 76, 78.

5. See Archibald Hart, *Children and Divorce* (Word Publishing, 1982) for a three-stage concept. Also see Patricia Papernow, who believes there are seven stages in blending a stepfamily: (1) fantasy, (2) assimilation, (3) awareness, (4) mobilization, (5) action, (6) contact, and (7) resolution. These seven stages are discussed in "A Phenomenological Study of the Developmental Stages of Becoming a Stepparent—A Gestalt and Family Systems Approach" (Ann Arbor, MI: University Microfilms International, 1980).

CHAPTER 2

Blended Family Birth Order 101

Why Firstborns Bump Heads in a Stepfamily

Whenever I conduct a birth order seminar, I can almost guarantee I'll get questions like these:

- "We have a blended family and now my firstborn son is really a middle child because my husband has a boy who is older than my son and a daughter who is younger. So what is he? Is he a firstborn or a middle child?"

- "I have married a woman who has three children who are all older than my daughter, who is an only child. Does that make her the baby of the family?"

What these people are really asking is, "If you wind up in a different birth order position in a blended family, does that mean you become that birth order?"

My answer is maybe yes, probably no. It depends on the *timing*.

If your family blends when the children are very young, well below the age of five or six, then the answer is yes. Someone who might have been born first in his original family could grow up more like a middle child, or even a baby, if that's where the new blending places him. For example, suppose little Rufus was born first in his original family but when he was two, his parents divorced and his mother quickly remarried a man with two other children, one of whom was three and a half and the other who was just ten months. In this case, little Rufus is almost certain to grow up with the characteristics of a middle child.

On the other hand, let us suppose little Rufus is born first, and his mother divorces when he's seven or eight. No matter what birth order position he takes in his blended family, he will always have a firstborn personality.

By the time a child is five or six years old, the grain of the wood is set. A firstborn is always a firstborn. Just because he suddenly has a stepbrother who is older, he doesn't stop being conscientious, goal oriented, or perfectionistic.

After age five or six, a middle child is always a middle child. She doesn't suddenly become a firstborn because her older sister went to live with her mother and now she's oldest in a new blended family. She remains someone who developed her life-style while feeling squeezed from above and below. The middle child can go in any direction. It just depends on how she branches off from an older brother or sister in her formative years.

And as for the inimitable baby of the family, he won't suddenly become a firstborn by nature just because he winds up oldest when divorce and remarriage create a new family structure. He is still a manipulative, charming, precocious, engaging little clown who likes to have fun and show off.

The point to remember is this: *When a child who is born into one birth order lands in another position in his blended family, do not treat the child as something he is not. He may have to take on different responsibilities or play different roles at times, but never forget who he really is.*

This principle is so important that I am spending the next four chapters going over the typical characteristics of each birth order to show you what happens when families blend and birth orders seem to change. Unless children are very young, their birth orders don't change, they collide. For a good illustration of what I'm talking about, we can't do any better than the family of firstborn Phil, whom you met in chapter 1.

Phil did come back to see me and he brought along his wife, Peggy. We spent an entire morning together, and it quickly became apparent where the pressure points were.

The first bit of bad news was that while Phil was a perfectionistic firstborn, Peggy was an only child because her mother couldn't have any more children. No wonder Peggy and Phil were having tension: He, a firstborn, was going head to head with an only child, a super firstborn, if you please, and no matter how much they loved each other, there had to be some sparks. And when they added their children to the mix, the sparks started flying faster.

Because Phil and Peggy both had custody of their children, theirs was a full-time blend. Phil had two children: Lance, sixteen; and Tiffany, fourteen. Added to that were Peggy's three children: Carol, sixteen; Patrick, fourteen; and Tina, ten. As I learned later in our session, Peggy's children went to see their father every other weekend and also spent at least a month with him during the summer.

Stepparenting Is No Picnic

By the time they were able to come to see me, Phil and Peggy had been married just over two years. As we talked together, Phil made it clear he wanted to pick up on something that he and I had discussed at lunch almost two months before.

"I did as you suggested," he reported. "In fact, we both have read *The Birth Order Book,* and while it has been very helpful, it doesn't explain why all the kids turned against our marriage so quickly. I recall that early on I suggested that we all sit down and have a family council, and my sixteen-year-old son, Lance, literally said, 'If it's going to be something that will help your marriage to her succeed, count me out. I'm not going to stab Mom in the back.'"

"That was really not an unusual remark for a stepchild to make, particularly a teenager like Lance," I explained. "Among counselors, a typical saying is, 'The stepfamily is born of loss.' Stepchildren don't get over their losses quickly. It can take years for them to get past all the grief and anger they're holding inside. Some of them carry that anger and pain around for life. That's why your son is rejecting your marriage and probably giving your wife a bad time in the bargain."

"Not probably—*definitely,*" Peggy interjected. "No matter how nice I try to be—I cook him his favorite dishes, I let him drive my car now and then—whatever it is, he's either coolly polite or he's critical."

"And it's my guess that you are feeling terrible about all this because you've tried so hard to step right in and do a great job of replacing Lance's mom, and hoping that he and Tiffany will respond with love in return."

Peggy didn't reply immediately, but from the look on her face, I could tell I was on target. Phil said, "You know, Peggy and I have sat up nights talking about what she can do to be accepted by my kids and what I can do to be accepted by hers. They give me a bad time, too, for the most part, so it isn't easy for either of us."

"In all the counseling I've done with blended families, I've found only a handful of cases where parents could love their stepchildren 'as if they were their own' and the stepchildren returned that love with all kinds of gusto. The fact is no stepparent can replace a natural parent, no matter how neglectful or abusive or inadequate that natural parent has been. In fact, in many cases, kids believe that their natural parent, who left the family for whatever reason, got a raw deal, and they want to see that natural parent as often as they can."

"Well, in our case, my ex-wife really doesn't want anything to do with my kids, and she contacts them maybe once or twice a year, usually with a card or a note. But Peggy's ex-husband lives in town, and we're on the typical visitation arrangement—he gets to see the kids every other weekend."

"Let me guess," I interjected. "Peggy, when your kids come back from those visits, you probably have all kinds of little problems and tensions—they butt heads with Lance and Tiffany and challenge you over the house rules."

"How did you know?" Peggy asked with surprise. "My ex-husband isn't much of a disciplinarian, and when they're with him, the kids stay up and watch movies we don't allow in our home. Of the three, Carol makes the adjustment pretty well, but Patrick and Tina are younger, and they take a few days to get back into the swing of things. In fact, that's when Patrick might bug Lance more than usual. So far, we've had them in the same room, but that's starting to wear pretty thin."

"If possible, it would be better for Lance to have his own room. At sixteen, a kid really likes his privacy," I commented.

"Fortunately, we're in the process of buying a bigger house," Phil offered. "For several reasons, we had to move into Peggy's house when we got married, even though we knew that wasn't the ideal thing to do. Having Lance and Patrick become roommates when they were fourteen and twelve didn't seem like too bad an idea, but now it's becoming a problem. Patrick can really be a pest—and he's a slob to boot. Frankly, I think I know how Lance feels. The other day he found a big mess that Patrick had made on his desk, and if I hadn't been home, there might have been bloodshed."

"If you'll remember my little blended family acrostic, B is for bloodshed, because a lot of people are walking around saying, 'Nobody's pushing me around!'" I reminded him.

"Well, I can certainly relate to that," Peggy sighed. "I've always had my problems with Tiffany, and she's really at odds with Tina, too. The one person Tiffany gets along with well is my son, Patrick. Maybe it's because they both play volleyball. They watch each other's games, give each other tips, tease each other over who's been winning—they seem to have a real connection."

"Tiffany and Tina are the youngest from each side of the family," I observed. "Are they sharing a bedroom?"

"Yes, they've also had to share a bedroom since Phil

and I were married. As Phil mentioned, we're buying a bigger house, so that's going to change, but right now there's a lot of tension between Tiffany and Tina. Tiffany tries to boss Tina around and doesn't like to share at all."

"I have daughters myself," I interjected. "Maybe Tina tries to borrow Tiffany's clothes or makeup sometimes?"

"Yes, that's right, and I don't know why Tiffany can't be a little more agreeable. Tina's always complaining about her attitude—she says Tiffany's mean to her."

Obviously, Peggy was being somewhat partial to her own daughter, but what she was telling me about Tiffany was no surprise. I had suspected that Tiffany might be a focal point of tension the minute we diagrammed their family. For at least twelve years she had been the baby of her original family and, no doubt, the apple of her daddy's eye.

Once the blend took place, Tiffany no longer held her Baby Princess position; now she not only had to compete with the precocious Tina, who was always stealing the spotlight, but she had to share a room with her as well! By Peggy's own admission, there were plenty of sparks flying between Tiffany and her stepmother, probably due to the fact that Peggy was a no-nonsense perfectionistic only child, and Tiffany, while enjoying the baby position in her family was also a firstborn girl who had picked up many of her father's perfectionistic ways.

Caution! Birth Order Variables at Work

As I talked with Phil and Peggy, I diagrammed their blended family and quickly spotted a major reason why they were having so much friction. As is often the case, an important phenomenon was at work, putting most of the family on a collision course.

When I had eaten lunch with Phil almost two months before, he had just heard me speak on birth order and had marveled at how I seemed to be able to describe everyone in his family "perfectly." What Phil didn't realize is that birth order is seldom as simple as "one, two, three, and everybody fits in their little slot." Being born first, second, last (or thirteenth), sets you up with some general tendencies and characteristics, but it doesn't guarantee that you're going to come out of some kind of birth order cookie cutter.

What really matters is the all-important factor of the dynamic relationships between you and the other members of your family. These relationships can be affected in any number of ways—what I call *birth order variables*. Actually, these variables are what make birth order theory really fascinating because they explain in great part why some people don't seem to fit the "mold" of their birth order.

As I speak on birth order in seminars and other settings around the country, most of the people who give me feedback are as amazed as Phil was. Because their children seem to fit the basic birth order categories to a tee, they think I'm some kind of clairvoyant or I've been tapping their phone or intercepting their mail.

But occasionally someone will tell me, "I'm a firstborn, and I'm not like what you described at all. I'm messy, never in control, and always disorganized." Or someone else might say, "I'm a last born, but I'm the one who's conscientious and perfectionistic. How do you explain that?"

In every crowd there are always examples of birth order inconsistencies, and I can almost always explain these with the concept of *birth order variables,* which include:

- the sex of each child (the order in which boys and girls arrive in the family)

- spacing (the number of years between children)

- physical differences (height, weight, illness, disability)

- the birth order of the parents (Birth order affects adults' style of parenting and also causes parents to identify with certain of their children better than others.)

- the blending of two or more families because of death or divorce (Blending, of course, is the biggest variable of all for any stepfamily, but other variables usually play an important part, as we shall see.)

In Phil and Peggy's family, two key variables were at work. First, Phil and Peggy were perfectionistic firstborn and only child personalities, and they both tended to approach the parenting task with a fault-finding attitude; second, the sex of their blended brood of five played an even more critical role in the kids' developing personalities.

How can the sex of each child make such a difference? For example, suppose a boy is born first, followed by a girl, and then another girl. Will they exhibit the typical firstborn, middle child, and last born characteristics? In many respects, they will, but you also have a firstborn male and a *firstborn female,* and she might come out with many firstborn characteristics of her own.

Or consider a family that consists of a boy, another boy, a girl, and another boy, all two years apart. Who do you think would get most of the attention in that family? The baby princess, of course. And who do you think might get short shrift? Yep, little last born caboose, baby prince. With two older brothers, he's nothing special, but his older sister is because she's the *only girl* in the family, the apple of her daddy's eye and the girl mommy always wanted after having to live with all those males.

When I diagrammed Phil and Peggy's family, the birth order variable of sex practically leaped off the page, as you will see below:

Phil (perfectionistic firstborn)	Peggy (special jewel only child)
Lance—16, firstborn boy	Carol—16, firstborn girl
Tiffany—14, firstborn girl	Patrick—14, firstborn boy
	Tina—10

As the diagram clearly shows, there were six people in Phil and Peggy's family with firstborn characteristics! That dynamic alone guaranteed there would be plenty bumping of heads. Peggy's problems with Lance and Tiffany weren't all due to the fact she was their stepmother. That played a part, true, but also affecting their relationship was the fact that they were all three firstborn personalities.

And Phil's problems with Patrick weren't all completely explained by stepdad-stepson friction. Both of them were firstborn personalities as well. The only firstborn who didn't have friction with the others was Peggy's daughter, Carol, and as I would learn a bit later, this was due largely to the fact that she was a compliant firstborn with many pleaser characteristics.

We'll get back to Phil and Peggy later in this chapter, but right here I would like to expand a bit on the characteristics of firstborns and only children and why they frequently compete or even clash in an intimate setting such as a blended family.

Firstborns Hit the Ground Running

With his parents as his only role models, the firstborn is constantly trying to emulate the all-powerful and all-knowing "giants" who seem to be able to do everything well and nothing wrong. Because they are so busy trying to imitate their much more capable parents, firstborns quite naturally tend to become careful planners who are detail oriented and well organized. They also tend to be serious, loyal, conscientious types who "can always be counted on." Firstborns often do well in school, developing self-reliance that makes them natural leaders.

Remember that as I list these "typical traits" of firstborns, I'm not saying that *all* firstborns have *all* of these traits. As we'll see in chapter 6, every person develops an individual way of looking at life and picks up certain characteristics that are unique to him or her.

Because a majority of my clients are firstborns, I've learned a lot about them over the years. Firstborns tend to be goal oriented achievers and self-sacrificing people pleasers. Because they are such careful planners, they are famous for making lists and getting all their ducks in a row. Firstborns don't like surprises. They also lean toward conservatism and are usually staunch supporters of law and order to the point that they can sometimes be legalistic. Not surprisingly, firstborns are highly respectful of authority and are strong believers in ritual and tradition.

I've already touched on the reason that firstborns develop these traits. Actually, there are two reasons: Mom and Dad. After all, this is their first shot at parenting; the firstborn is their guinea pig. Ironically, while they tend to be overprotective, anxious, tentative, and inconsistent with their firstborn child, at the same time they'll usually be very strict and demanding, always pushing and encouraging more and better performance.

Firstborns Come in Two Basic Models

With all this pressure from parents, it sounds as if firstborns would be strong-willed and aggressive, but that's hardly the case. Many firstborns are hard-driving achievers, but many others are compliant and eager to please in addition to being achievement oriented.

The compliant firstborn has a strong need for approval. That's why a firstborn may be so conscientious, so willing to toe the mark, obey the rules, and get good grades. This kid's a firstborn, all right, but she is driven by her pleaser nature. A good example of a compliant firstborn is Carol, Peggy's oldest child, whose desire to be liked and approved of kept her out of most of the firstborn battles raging around her.

One of the most pleasing, nurturing, and care-giving firstborns I know is my wife, Sande. And one of the best choices I, a last born, ever made was to make her my wife. Long before I had ever heard of birth order, I paired off with the perfect match for me (explained more fully in chapter 7).

On the flip side, assertive, hard-driving firstborns can have personalities like badgers or pit bulls. They come on strong because they have to achieve, win, control—in short, be kingpin. The assertive, hard-driving firstborn leaves little to chance and wants to know all the facts.

While firstborns receive more discipline than any other birth order, they get the long end of the stick in some positive ways, too. One of the perks of being firstborn is that anything you do is a big deal as far as Mom and Dad (and the rest of the family, for that matter) are concerned. Everyone tends to take firstborns very seriously, and firstborns try to live up to their confident, responsible image, often becoming leaders, managers, or administrators.

"Will All the Firstborn Accountants Please Stand"

Firstborns often enter exacting professions, such as accounting. On one occasion I was invited to speak to a statewide gathering of certified public accountants in America's heartland. I was given the typical glowing introduction, but when I came to the podium I didn't say all the right things, such as "It's nice to be here," or "It's a privilege to speak to a group like this."

Instead, the first words out of my mouth were, "Would all of you firstborns and only children in the room please stand up."

These CPAs looked at one another as if to say, "Who is *this?*" It took a few seconds, but finally *almost everyone in the room* rose to his or her feet.

"Thank you very much," I said, "please take your seats. Now, will those who did not rise please stand at this time."

I had already counted the house, so I knew that there were 221 people in the room—every one of them an accountant. And when I asked for the second group—

all those who were *not* firstborns or only children—to stand, it was easy to count them—because only *nineteen* people got up!

I quickly counted them, paused for another long moment, and finally said, "What are you doing *here?*"

There was a roar of laughter, and our evening was off to a relaxed and amusing start—no small feat with over two hundred CPAs, who by nature are anything but a barrel of laughs.

Presidents and Pastors Are Often Firstborns

The statistics on firstborns in positions of high authority or achievement are well known. Look in *Who's Who in America* or *American Men and Women of Science* and you will find a high percentage of firstborns. The same is true of Rhodes scholars and university professors.[1]

I did a little research recently and learned that, up to and including George W. Bush, twenty-four out of forty-three U.S. presidents (56 percent) have been firstborns, yet only five (14 percent) have been only borns or the oldest son in the family: Andrew Jackson, William Henry Harrison, Andrew Johnson, James Garfield, and the ex-actor and entertainer, Ronald Reagan.[2] (It is worth noting that Nancy, the former president's only-child wife, calls him "Ronnie.")

And for the record, ten presidents came from stepfamilies, including George Washington, Martin Van Buren, Franklin Pierce, Abraham Lincoln, Benjamin Harrison, William Taft, Calvin Coolidge, Franklin Roosevelt, Gerald Ford, and Bill Clinton.[3]

Another profession loaded with firstborns is the pastorate. While speaking on birth order to a group of fifty ministers, I commented, "Pastors, you know, are predominantly firstborns."

There they sat, arms akimbo, legs crossed, skeptical looks on their faces as if I had pronounced some kind of heresy. So, I went for it:

"Okay, I could be wrong, but let's find out. Sir, your birth order?"

The first person I asked was a firstborn son, so was the second. I went down the line and didn't hit a middle or last born until the eighth man. I went ahead with the entire group, and forty-three out of fifty were firstborn sons or only children.

Lonely Onlies Get a Bad Rap

And maybe this is a good time to comment that the only child, first cousin to a firstborn, has all of the same characteristics—*in spades*. To put it another way, an only child is a *super* firstborn—super-perfectionistic, super-achieving, super-conscientious, and super-organized, to name a few of the firstborn traits that only children take to new frontiers. I like to tell seminar crowds that you can always tell an only child in the kindergarten milk line: all the other kids are holding their Batman or Barney lunch pails while he clutches his attaché case!

Because only children don't have the problem of learning to share with siblings, a lot of people think they are selfish hedonists or self-centered narcissists. Alfred Adler, the father of birth order theories, didn't think much of only children either. He said, "The only child has difficulties with every independent activity and sooner or later they become useless in life."[4]

I'm sure Alfie must have had a bad day with an only

child when he made that observation. Many only children have been high achievers who could be called anything but useless. Just a few who have come out in fairly good shape include Franklin D. Roosevelt, Leonardo da Vinci, Sarah Ferguson (the Duchess of Windsor), Charles Lindbergh, and Indira Gandhi.

Other successful only children include Ted Koppel, Dick Cavett, Lena Horne, Lauren Bacall, Brooke Shields, and leading football stars such as Roger Staubach, Joe Montana, and Thurman Thomas. Two other very successful only children are internationally known business tycoons Carl Icahn and T. Boone Pickens.

Another profession loaded with firstborns and only children is talk show hosts. During a tour of thirty-one cities, I did a little survey and discovered that out of ninety-two talk show hosts, only five were not firstborns or onlies. Besides onlies Ted Koppel and Dick Cavett, other well-known talk show personalities who are firstborns or only children include Phil Donahue, Oprah Winfrey, Sonja Friedman, Geraldo Rivera, Arsenio Hall, Sally Jessy Raphael, and the spokesman for Excellence in Broadcasting himself, Rush Limbaugh.

It is interesting to note that more and more of today's families are opting to have only one child. According to the U.S. Census Bureau, between 1980 and 1990 there was a 76 percent increase among women near the end of childbearing years who still had only one child. In other words, there was a very good chance that these families would have no more children.[5]

At the same time, the only child is getting better press, and more recent research indicates that only children aren't doomed to be neurotics, narcissists, or useless nincompoops. A social psychologist who teaches at the University of Texas in Austin says, "The view of only children as selfish and lonely is a gross exaggeration of reality."[6]

According to a family therapist from Brigham Young University, research shows that only borns have great initiative, enjoy high self-esteem, and don't call themselves lonely.[7]

Why Is She an Only Child?

One of the keys to understanding the only child is to ask *why* she is the only one. If she is a special jewel because her parents wanted other children and couldn't have any more, then she might wind up with the feeling that she's the center of the universe. But if she's an only child because her parents planned it that way, her cool, confident exterior may be covering up a frightened, rebellious, angry person who is hard on herself and her peers.

You may recall that Peggy, Phil's wife, was a "special jewel" only child because her mother couldn't have any more children. Because she grew up as the center of her family's universe, Peggy found it extremely difficult to understand the ungrateful and even hostile responses of her stepdaughter, Tiffany, and her stepson, Lance. A sweet and gentle pleaser by nature, Peggy had always known success and acceptance in just about everything she did. Becoming a stepmother had thrown her for a loop—and then some.

And even before becoming part of a blended family, Peggy, an only child, had some problems with parenting. She could not understand why her children squabbled so much. How could she? She hadn't grown up with the "benefit" of having to interact, argue, share, and compete with other siblings. Whenever I counsel only children, they often tell me, "I don't understand why my kids are always fighting."

My own research and study of firstborns and only children show that either position has its perks, but it also has at least one big problem—pressure. Firstborns and onlies are under the gun from day one, continually admonished to sit up straight, shape up, do it now, take charge, and be an example.

After I wrote *Growing Up Firstborn,* I got a lot of feedback from firstborn and only children concerning the book's subtitle, "The Pressure and Privilege of Being Number One." Wherever I went to speak and teach, firstborns and only children would say, "There was plenty of pressure, all right, but what's this about privilege? Being number one is mostly pressure."

This firstborn "the glass is half empty" view of pressure and privilege is not too surprising. Because of their uncanny ability to spot flaws wherever they may appear, firstborns tend to see the glass half empty more often than they see it half full. The home of Phil and Peggy was no exception, where six firstborn personalities were trying to learn how to coexist.

Phil and Peggy: A Firstborn Free-for-All

As Peggy described her tensions with Phil's daughter, Tiffany, I watched him to see if I could detect a reaction. He listened carefully, and although he winced a few times as Peggy described Tiffany's attitude, he seemed to take it all fairly well. Because I was curious about what Phil thought about Peggy's analysis, I asked him what he saw in Tiffany's relationship with Tina, her stepsister, as well as with Peggy.

"Well, I haven't really been around that much when they're together," Phil said slowly. "Maybe Tiffany does get a little pushy. Because she had asthma as a small child, she was treated special from the start, and to be honest, I guess I've always kept it up. She and I are very close."

As Phil continued to talk, he admitted, however, that he didn't feel all that close to his stepson, Patrick, the volleyball star who worked just hard enough on his studies to stay eligible.

"I have trouble getting on Patrick's wavelength," Phil admitted. "His casual approach to schoolwork bothers me, and his messiness hasn't helped either. I don't blame Lance for getting irritated with him—you should smell his dirty socks, which he often leaves lying around their bedroom. But getting back to Tiffany for a second, I'm really worried about her, too, but for other reasons. She was a fairly decent student until about two years ago, when Peggy and I got married. Now her grades have dropped way off, and sometimes I think if she didn't have volleyball she wouldn't want to go to school at all."

"The fact that Tiffany and Patrick both play volleyball has its pluses and minuses," Peggy interjected. "At least they get along well together, but the downside is that they sometimes gang up on Tina. Patrick has never liked his little sister that much—he has always called her a pest."

"I'm not singling out Tiffany as the troublemaker in the family," I stressed to Phil, "but I believe what you and Peggy must try to do is 'get behind her eyes,' so to speak, and see things the way she is seeing them. She's always been very special, and now that's no longer true because she's got a lot of competition from precocious little Tina. I agree that it's a positive thing that she is volleyball buddies with Patrick, but it's a negative that they get together and gang up on Tina. Tell me, does Tiffany seem competitive with Carol as well as Tina?"

"They don't cross swords, but I wouldn't say there is a lot of warmth between them," Peggy told me. "Carol is a junior in high school and has her own schedule, her own friends—in fact, she just began dating a few months ago. She and Tiffany just don't seem to find a lot of time for each other."

While sorting out all of the birth order collisions in the family, I had forgotten about an obvious combination. I asked Peggy, "We've been so busy talking about the younger kids, I'm wondering how Lance and Carol, the two firstborns, get along. In a blended family, the closer children are in age, the more likely they are to bump heads. Lance and Carol are both sixteen. Do they clash?"

"From my perspective, I'd say no," Phil answered. "Lance plays football—first-string tackle on the JV team last fall—and he hits the books pretty hard. He's really interested in getting into a good college. Carol is more into music and drama. In fact, in that respect she's much like her mom, wouldn't you say that's true, Peggy?"

"Yes, I think that's quite true," Peggy agreed. "We've given Carol piano lessons since she was quite young, and dancing lessons, too. She's been in several plays at school and seems to have some real talent. She also has a very sweet, easygoing way about her."

"That doesn't surprise me," I said. "Carol sounds like a compliant pleaser, which is one of the obvious reasons why she and Lance don't collide that much. It also helps that they're different sexes—that makes them less competitive as well. And when you add the fact that they have different interests, with each one occupying a much different 'turf,' so to speak, you can see that neither one threatens the other. Here, at least, you don't have two firstborns the same age going at it, which is a plus."

"Well, Lance may not bump heads with Carol, but he does with me," Peggy admitted. "No matter what I do to be a loving stepmother, he won't forgive me for replacing his mom, who pretty well deserted him and seldom contacts him at all. And I'm not having much luck with Tiffany, either. I have to admit I'm not the world's greatest housekeeper, and she gets all over me when a room isn't picked up or a pair of her favorite jeans gets temporarily misplaced in the laundry. Of course, I remind her that she isn't too neat with her part of the room she shares with Tina. And she's not that nice to Tina either."

"So, the bottom line is that you often feel like the wicked stepmother?"

"Even worse, I often feel like a failure," Peggy said as a tear glistened. "My son, Patrick, is always fighting with Phil's son, Lance; my youngest daughter, Tina, is always fighting with Phil's daughter, Tiffany. Sometimes I feel like a referee. Everyone is depending on me to keep the family on an even keel, and I'm just not cutting it."

At this point I suggested that we take a break and have a cup of coffee. Peggy's admittance that she felt as if everyone were depending on her was the cry of a typical firstborn or only child. As I counsel firstborns or super firstborns, I also hear them saying, usually with a sigh or even with a snort of anger, things like:

- "I can't get away with anything."

- "It was tough being the oldest [or the only one]."

- "I was never allowed to be a child."

- "Why does everyone depend on *me*?"

Positive and Negative Aspects of Being a Firstborn or Only Child

Firstborn Trait	Positive Aspect	Negative Aspect
Perfectionistic	Does everything well	Overly critical and dissatisfied with his own performance
Driven	Ambitious, headed for success	Always under great pressure
Organized	Able to stay on top of everything	No room in his life for flexibility
Scholarly	Able to think problems through and solve them	Sometimes thinks too much, is overly serious
List-Driven	Gets things done; knows where he's going	Boxes himself in; becomes a slave to his "to-do" list
Logical	Avoids pitfalls of compulsive behavior	Knows he's right, even when he isn't
Leader	Plays an important part in his family, community, etc.	Expected to do too much; always leaned on by others
Compliant	Known as a "good guy"	Known as an "easy mark"
Aggressive	Gets ahead in life; others look up to him	Tends to be selfish and to disregard the feelings of others

- "If I don't do it, it won't get done."

- "If I don't do it, it won't get done *right*."

- "I know I could have done it better!"

While Peggy hadn't used the phrase, "I could have done it better," it was obvious she was thinking it. Peggy, the only child, and Phil, her meticulous firstborn husband, were both carrying the same burden, which we will examine more closely in chapter 3.

NOTES

1. "What Scholars, Strippers, and Congressmen Share," a study by Richard Zweigenhaft, reported by Jack Horn, *Psychology Today*, May 1976, 34.

2. Joseph Nathan Kane, *Facts About the Presidents: From George Washington to Bill Clinton* (New York: The H.W. Wilson Company, 1993). Information about George W. Bush found on www.infoplease.com/spot/georgewbush1.html; accessed 2/14/01.

3. Kane, *Facts About the Presidents*.

4. Alfred Adler, *Understanding Human Nature* (New York: Fawcett World Library, 1969), 127.

5. Karen Peterson, "Kids Without Siblings Get Their Due," *USA Today*, March 1, 1993, 1D.

6. "Only Children: Cracking the Myth of the Pampered Lonely Misfit," *U.S. News and World Report*, January 10, 1994, 50.

7. Peterson, "Kids Without Siblings Get Their Due," 2D.

CHAPTER 3

Blended Family Birth Order 102

Perfectionism— Deadly Enemy of the Stepfamily

As a counselor, I treat a dangerous disease that infects millions of people in every corner of the earth. It's not the common cold, cancer, heart disease, or AIDS. I refer to another sickness, which many people ironically think is a badge of honor: *perfectionism*. While perfectionists can be found in other birth orders (particularly middle children), perfectionism is the dominating burden of almost all firstborns and only children. Perfectionism haunts them like the headless horseman haunted Sleepy Hollow.

"I know I could have done it better," is a telltale sign of the firstborn or only child who is carrying what I call the albatross of perfectionism around his neck.

One of my favorite examples of perfectionism is a personal ad I clipped out of a daily newspaper. I have shared it in other books,[1] but it's worth repeating here to demonstrate the length to which perfectionists try to go:

Christian, blond, blue eyes, 5′2″, 100 lbs., prof., cauc/female, no depend., wishes to meet Protestant Christian, prof. man in 30s with college degree who has compassion for animals and people, loves nature, exercise and phy. fitness *(no team sports)*, music and dance, church and home life. Desire nonsmoker/nondrinker, slender, 5′7″–6′, lots of head hair, *no chest hair,* intelligent, honest and trustworthy, sense of humor, excellent communicator of feelings, very sensitive, gentle, affectionate, androgynous attitude about roles, giving, encouraging and helpful to others, *no temper or ego problems,* secure within and financially, health conscious, neat and clean, extremely considerate and dependable. I believe in old-fashioned morals and values. If you do, too, and are interested in a possible Christian commitment, write to PO Box 82533. Please include recent color photo and address.

I italicized a few phrases in the above ad to illustrate how demanding a perfectionist can be. It's my guess that this blond, blue-eyed Christian lady was a divorcée who was trying to find Mr. Right the second time around. I have no idea whether she did, but I'm willing to go out on a limb and suggest that she will probably be single for a long time. Perhaps it is just as well because if this woman wound up in a blended family, Christian as she may claim to be, it would really be a mess. The obvious reason: No one could live with her for more than a day, if that long. Her intolerance could drive everyone in the family to drink!

You see, it's little things like team sports that drive the perfectionist crazy, and they in turn drive others crazy with their nit-picking, which can often be very subtle. Parents—especially stepparents—should be aware that being picky is a deadly destroyer of motivation—and of children. I can recall counseling a girl of thirteen who described her relationship with her stepmother by saying, "No matter what I do to help her, it's never quite good enough. She just does it over, so what's the use?"

Games Perfectionists Play

I often tell my clients that perfectionism is slow suicide. If you are a perfectionist, remember that your disease can kill any marriage. Above all, it can kill you. Perfectionists usually wonder what is driving them down the road to destruction. If you were paying attention when you read about firstborns and only children, you know the answers: trying to imitate Mom and Dad, not to mention carrying the burdens that every firstborn knows all too well—being in the limelight, being the most responsible, and always having to set an example. Any firstborn is familiar with lines like these:

- "You don't want to take little brother with you. Fine. You can just stay home."

- "Now remember, you've got to act your age!"

- "I don't care what *she* did. *You* are the oldest! I expect more out of you, young lady."

- "So he started it. That doesn't give you any excuse to belt somebody who is so much smaller than you are!"

- "I'm really disappointed. I was depending on you to set an example."

With all these responsibilities and constant admonishments, it's no wonder that firstborn perfectionists grow up having the tendency to bite off more than they can chew. One of the favorite games perfectionists like to play could be called "Of course I can handle it!" The *it* in question could be anything from an impossible task to adding just one more responsibility—and that one responsibility could be the straw that breaks the perfectionist's back.

Another favorite perfectionist game is called "It's all or nothing." In other words, the perfectionist has to be the best, do the most, work the longest. They put their goals ahead of everything, including their need for recreation, time with their family, or time to get sufficient rest.

Biting off more than he can chew added to all or nothing thinking often ensnares the perfectionist in a third game called "I'll never be able to get all this done!"

When counseling perfectionists I usually find they are overwhelmed by the big picture. Initially, they just can't seem to break down their overwhelming problem. Later, they may use their considerable powers of organization to figure it all out, but that victory usually comes at a price, paid by their stomachs as well as by those who have to live with them.

The perfectionist typically sets too many goals or sets them too high. The result is the perfect setup for getting overwhelmed by the big picture. Some counselors call this the *hurdle effect* because as the perfectionist looks down the road and sees so many roadblocks and hurdles ahead, she feels defeated.[2] When this happens, it's typical of the perfectionist to back off or back out of what she has committed to do. Another response is to procrastinate and wait until the last minute, then do a rush job and excuse the results by saying, "I just didn't have enough time."

Another favorite game of the perfectionist has already been mentioned: "It's okay, I guess—it could be better." Playing this game leads to the debilitating practice of *maximizing and minimizing,* that is, maximize your failures and minimize your successes.[3] No matter what the perfectionist does, she will make a lot out of her mistakes and imperfections and very little out of her accomplishments and achievements.

I call this impossible standard the high jump bar of life, which perfectionists can whip out at a moment's notice to judge themselves or others. Instead of being happy with a good effort, they measure it against their ever present high jump bar and say, "With a little more time, it could have been great!"

And all of this leads the perfectionist to one other game best described as "I must try harder." The perfectionist is the original victim of the Avis Complex, always feeling he's number two or lower, always trying to be better, never satisfied that what he has done is good enough, even if others tell him it's outstanding. Numerous celebrities and people normally thought to have been geniuses in their respective professions were perfectionists who were haunted by the Avis Complex:

- Actor Alec Guinness said, "I'm very insecure about my work. I've never done anything I couldn't pull to bits."

- After presenting his Gettysburg Address, Abraham Lincoln described it as "a flat failure."

- Actress Elizabeth Taylor once gave this opinion of her ability: "I hate to see myself on the screen. I hate the way I look. I hate the sound of my voice. I'm always thinking I should have played it better."

- Leonardo da Vinci, one of the most talented human beings who ever lived, said, "I've offended God and mankind because my work didn't reach the quality it should have."[4]

And so the perfectionist goes round and round in a hopeless pursuit of perfection (see the diagram on p. 51). Fortunately, it is possible for perfectionists to reform. I have received a letter from a woman who was born third in her family, but because of the accidental deaths of her older brother and sister, she was reared as an only child for most of the first seven years of her life. She became a perfectionist with a deep fear of failure and was very hard on herself for past mistakes.

This woman doesn't like to be in charge in situations involving other people. She believes she is timid and shy but says that when she's sure about something she is very bold and takes a strong stand. She's describing a typical trait of the only child or firstborn. Firstborn perfectionists are known for tiptoeing into things, but once sure of their ground they will make it chapter and verse for their lives.

It's encouraging to note that after marrying, having two children, and being left a single mother because of divorce, this woman underwent a spiritual renewal that changed her life. "I was one of those irritating perfectionists who made everyone around me miserable," she writes. "Now people who know me have trouble believing I was that way. My home is clean and comfortable and 'lived in,' no longer a shrine to my sense of control."[5]

The Hopeless Pursuit
of Perfection[6]

1. "It's all or nothing. I must be perfect."

2. "There is nothing I can't do or accomplish."

3. "How did I get into this? I'll never be able to get it all done."

4. "It could have been better . . . I blew it again!"

5. "I am what I do . . . the only thing that counts is results—performance!"

6. "I'll try harder—I know I can do better than that!"

How Perfectionistic Are You?

Let's stop right now and take a quick quiz to see if you fall into the category of mild perfectionist, medium perfectionist, or severe perfectionist (severe with everything and everyone, particularly yourself). To score your test, fill in the blank next to each question with 0 for *never,* 1 for *seldom,* 2 for *often,* and 3 for *always.*

_____ 1. Do you get irritated with mistakes—your own or someone else's?

_____ 2. Do you feel everyone should always do his best, always give 110 percent?

_____ 3. Do you often "should" yourself—in other words, do you tell yourself you should do this or shouldn't do that?

_____ 4. Do you get down on yourself when you fail or make a mistake?

_____ 5. Do you dislike the idea of being "average"?

_____ 6. Do you procrastinate and then make the excuse that you didn't have time to do things right?

_____ 7. Do you find it hard to finish a project because you know it can be better?

_____ 8. When working with others, do you tend to take over and control the situation?

_____ 9. Are you a creature of habit who wants all your ducks in a row?

_____10. Do you see the glass half empty instead of half full?

A score of 10 or less means you're a mild perfectionist. Between 10 and 20 pegs you as a medium perfectionist. If you scored 20 to 30, you're a severe perfectionist and you're being too hard on yourself and everyone around you. One other question to ask yourself is, "Do I feel guilty a great deal of the time?" If guilt is a real problem for you, it will probably be reflected in your perfectionism score. In other words, the more guilt, the higher the degree of perfectionism.

Phil and Peggy Were Extreme Perfectionists

After our coffee break, I gave the perfectionist quiz to Phil and Peggy. He scored 22, and she scored 25! Of the two, Peggy felt the most guilt because she had a pleaser life-style, feeling that unless she made everybody happy she was a failure. (There's more on life-styles in chapter 6.) Phil felt some guilt for the way things were going in his blended family, but for him the more evident emotions were frustration and even anger.

Because he wanted to be the best stepfather he could, he had tried to extend himself to Carol, Patrick, and Tina, but two things had backfired right in Phil's face. First, the only one who gave him much encouragement at all was Carol, who had always been ignored by her dad. Carol wanted a father very much, and she enjoyed Phil's attention. Also, natural sibling rivalry took over to some extent when Carol saw her younger brother, Patrick, turning Phil off. Patrick's negative response encouraged her all the more to open up to her stepdad.

But when Phil paid any special attention to Carol— attending one of her plays at school, for example—Tiffany gave him the cold shoulder. That behavior was bad enough, but if he showed any interest in Tina, Tiffany hit the roof, telling him that he was unfair and that he really didn't love her after all.

If Phil felt guilty about his attitude toward anyone, it was Patrick, whom he'd already described as someone who drove him a little crazy with his sloppiness and poor study habits. Nor was Phil happy with Patrick's continual complaints about having to go to bed early after getting back from his dad's house, where he got to stay up late and watch all the HBO movies he wanted.

"Phil, remember the blended family myths we talked about when we first met at lunch?" Phil nodded and I went on: "Almost all blended families buy into the big myth that they'll be different—they'll make it work and have no problems. Not only that, but they think it's all going to happen instantly. As a businessman, Phil, you may be thinking that all this is a black and white issue—that blending a family is like a business deal. Because you're having trouble, you're feeling as if you've failed, and that's making you feel guilty. You've got to remember that if there is anything that isn't black and white, it's a blended family. So be patient, color your blended family gray, and hang in there. People aren't like business deals. Feelings aren't like specifications and printouts. There's no way to sign everybody on the dotted line to live happily ever after."

Can a Firstborn Perfectionist Be a Slob?

As for Peggy the pleaser, she reminded me to some extent of the discouraged perfectionist who might claim that she wasn't perfectionistic at all—and to prove it all she had to do was point to her messy desk or her messy kitchen. Peggy was far from being a slob, but she admittedly didn't keep a perfect house, and this "shortcoming" made her a target for Tiffany's tirades over the rooms that weren't quite picked up and laundry that didn't get done.

Whenever I try to explain discouraged perfectionists, I remind people of a cardinal rule of birth order: Where you enter the family zoo (I call it that for obvious reasons) is only a start. How you interact with the environment of your particular family zoo is what is all-important.

It's true that all firstborns aren't neat as a pin and color coordinated. Some could win Mr. Blackwell's "worst dressed" prize hands down. But the reason they're sloppy or frumpy is that they are *discouraged* perfectionists. When they were little, they tried to live up to the standards set by Mom or Dad or other adults, but they just couldn't handle it. It was easier, therefore, to become sloppy and to ignore the perfectionistic tapes that kept playing in their heads.

When Peggy told me that her parents had both been firstborns and were "very strict about everything," it was easy to see where her own perfectionism had come from. I pointed out to her that as I counsel perfectionists, I have found that most of them have a messy spot or two in their lives but they are still perfectionists nonetheless. Perfectionists find "order within the disorder." This helped explain why Peggy didn't worry too much about keeping a perfect house but could still be called a perfectionist. Her private desk was littered with piles of bills, notes, and unopened mail, but she still knew where everything was and, even though Phil was the businessman of the family, it was Peggy who kept the checkbook in meticulous order.

Confessions of Edwin
the Perfectionist

Peggy and Phil were both quite surprised by their high scores on my perfectionist quiz, but I told them not to be chagrined. They had made an important discovery about how to deal more effectively in blending their family. Becoming aware of your perfectionism is the first step toward getting rid of that albatross around your neck—or at least turning it into a dove or a sparrow. I'm always pleased when someone writes to tell me I've made them more aware of something they've been bothered by or wondering about for years. Such was the case with Edwin. I quote almost all of his letter only because it is so indicative of an enlightened perfectionist:

> Can't remember when I laughed so much while reading a non-fiction book. Laughed? I howled at some paragraphs in The Birth Order Book. And then I threw the book across the room when you answered a question that has been bugging me for years.

> So, this is a thank-you letter for answering, in fact, several questions that have haunted me for a long time. And, especially, for forcing me to realize a few things about myself and my relationship with friends and co-workers. Also, I wanted to alert you to something my friends and I have discovered.

> Want clues to my birth order? I bought your book after wandering into a New York bookstore last Saturday, while fretting that the scarf I purchased a month earlier was navy blue—not black as I thought—and didn't match my new black top coat. I'm a former newspaper reporter; now one of five vice presidents with a publicly traded telecommunications company.

If that's not enough: in my closet, dress shirts are on blue hangers, dark shirts on the left, lighter-colored shirts on the right; sport shirts are on brown hangers. I'm laughing so much thinking about this, I can hardly continue writing.

Surely you've guessed: I have no siblings. But here's something curious that I discovered several years ago and wanted to alert you to: Virtually all of my close friends are firstborn or only children. And with two exceptions, all fall in the much-younger, much-older groups—something that has always been apparent to me, but I never understood until reading your book.

Of course, I've always known that I was not a perfectionist—far from it. Proof: my desk has, throughout my career, been a mess most of the time (but I can find anything within sixty seconds). And then I read your book and converted it into a Frisbee! I could never figure out why I lost control of my desk so often. Thank you for telling me the answer to something that has bugged me for years.

Nonetheless, it is a bit spooky having a stranger— you—know so much about my personal life. Good grief.

Also, thank you for explaining why my father never seemed happy with the last twenty years of his career. You see, he was the third child—the baby. However, his father died shortly after he was born, and his mother remarried, giving birth to my favorite aunt about four years later. (From her I learned that one should alphabetize the spices in the kitchen cabinet—again, I am now suffering from uncontrollable laughter.)

My father became a . . . , well, you already know. He was so successful that he was promoted to general manager. Through his dedication to work, we had a very comfortable life-style. But he wasn't especially happy with his job. After reading your book, I realize he would have much rather been selling the cars than running the place. Incidentally, his wardrobe leaned more toward Brooks Brothers than Las Vegas pit boss . . . probably because when I was in my early teens I began picking out his clothes. He just didn't understand things, like you don't wear a navy blue scarf with a black top coat.

Dr. Leman, you will never know how much enlightenment your book has given me. Thank you.[7]

Seeking Excellence vs. Pursuing Perfectionism

I treasure a letter like Edwin's, not just because he gives me some nice strokes but because he has learned some things about himself and will be able to make some changes for the better. At least he will be able to understand why he does certain things and not be so puzzled or frustrated.

One frustration many perfectionists have centers around this question: "Well, if I'm not supposed to try for perfection, what am I supposed to do? Do worse than my best and just live a mediocre life?"

I always answer, "Not at all. Instead, learn the difference between pursuing perfectionism and seeking excellence." The following quiz will help you sort out the difference between your own interpretations of perfectionism vs. excellence. Simply put an *E* (for excellence) or a *P* (for perfectionism) in front of each statement.

_____ 1. *I strive to do my best.*

_____ 2. *I aim for the top.*

_____ 3. I tell myself "I want" or "I would like."

_____ 4. I tell myself "I should" or "I must."

_____ 5. I am motivated by the desire for success.

_____ 6. I am motivated by a deep fear of failure.

_____ 7. I enjoy the process involved in what I make or manage or the service I do.

_____ 8. I focus on the product—results are what count.

_____ 9. I try to meet high standards to do the best I can.

_____10. My high standards help me outdo everyone else.

_____11. Life is a daily challenge.

_____12. Life is a daily battle.

_____13. When I finish a job, I feel accomplishment and fulfillment.

_____14. When I finish a job, I don't take time to enjoy it—I just look forward to the next project or task.

_____15. I realize that nobody's perfect.

_____16. I believe that perfection is a worthwhile goal as long as it's kept under control.

Odd numbered statements identify someone who seeks excellence; even numbered statements identify a perfectionist. If you are in a blended family, make seeking excellence your goal. Forget about perfection because it simply isn't within reach.

In a stepfamily, perfectionism will set you up for self-doubt and misery because you will think you are valued for what you do rather than for who you are. If you seek perfectionism in your stepfamily, the failures and disappointments that are bound to come will defeat and depress you. But if you settle for seeking excellence, you can accept disappointment and keep going. Remember, failure devastates the perfectionist, but failure is a teacher and a real help to the seeker of excellence.

Rare is the stepfamily in which a stepparent isn't criticized. If you're seeking perfectionism, you will hate the criticism (and probably the critics). If you're seeking excellence, you're more apt to welcome criticism. You may not enjoy it, but you can accept it and learn from it.

Tips for Firstborn or Only Child Perfectionists

Some general advice that I gave to Phil and Peggy included two basic principles that pertain to stepparenting no matter what birth order you might be or what kind of personality you have.

First, when your stepchildren rebuff you, remember that you're in this for the long haul. Don't expect instant results, and, above all, remember that your stepchildren are the children and you are the adult. That should give you an edge (even when you're bleeding a little inside). Peggy, with her desire to make everyone happy, needed to know that stepparenting is a two-steps-forward-one-step-backward proposition; she should not take her stepchildren's rejections so personally.

Second, as a stepparent, determine that you are going to love your spouse's kids, no matter what. For Phil, that meant being willing to arouse the anger of his own children, particularly Tiffany, who was having birth order rumbles with Patrick and Tina and didn't want to share her dad with anyone.

No matter what your birth order—firstborn, only child, or something else, it's possible that you are a perfectionistic stepparent, and that being true, it's likely you are experiencing friction with your stepchildren. Here are a few other don'ts and some do's for perfectionistic stepmoms or stepdads:

1. *Don't be so picky* with your spouse, your stepkids, your own kids, and yourself. Good advice for any perfectionist is this: If you must make a constructive criticism, do it only after giving two or three compliments. And when making *any* suggestion or observation, it's always a good idea to say, "I could be wrong, but . . ."

2. *Don't ask so many questions,* especially questions beginning with the word *why.* Wanting all the facts, details, and reasons is a telltale firstborn, only child trait, and it was one of Phil's major weaknesses. I told him that kids—especially teenagers like Patrick—really don't like to be put on the spot. In fact, no one does and that's the reason the word *why* can be so deadly.

3. *Don't try to "do it all."* As I advised Peggy, "Learn to say no because no matter how hard you try, you'll never please everyone anyway, particularly your stepkids."

When possible (and advisable), don't hesitate to give your stepchildren appropriate responsibilities—chores—that can lighten your own load. Always try to do it pleasantly, with a smile, and remember that no one person in the family is more important than the whole group (more on this in chapter 9).

4. *Do be willing to laugh at your mistakes.* Always try to find the humor in the situation, but be especially

cautious about giving your stepkids the impression you are laughing at them. Only children usually have a combination of firstborn and last born traits, and they can often have a keen sense of humor that leans toward satire or sarcasm. As I talked with Peggy, I detected this to be the case, and I encouraged her to be careful about using humor with even the gentlest bite in it around her stepkids, especially Tiffany.

5. *Do lighten up and lower your expectations.* I told Phil and Peggy, "Take whatever you expect from yourself and your stepkids, cut it in half, and then, if need be, cut it in half again." Perfectionists sometimes worry about compromising themselves if they "lower their standards." If they're true perfectionists, they needn't worry. Even if they cut their expectations in half, there will be plenty left!

6. *Do try to be more positive.* Perfectionists are notorious pessimists. Both Phil and Peggy had this problem, but in different ways; he from the meticulous controller's stance, she from the compliant pleaser's point of view. My advice to them: "When tempted to see the glass half empty, make a conscious effort to remind yourself that there are always positives in any situation."

Perfectionists Skate on Thin Ice

The reason I've devoted a substantial amount of space to perfectionism is because it can be a deadly enemy in any family—particularly the blended family. If you are an only child or a firstborn who has any perfectionistic traits at all, be aware that your perfectionism could be a major cause of any friction you are having with your stepchildren and, worse, your spouse.

As a perfectionist, you may think it's perfectly normal

to alphabetize the spice rack, cover the furniture with sheets except on Christmas and Easter, and color coordinate everything and everyone in sight, but the people you live with probably don't. Your tendency to pick flaws and criticize can unblend a family faster than almost anything else.

That concludes our study of Blended Family Birth Order 101 and 102, covering firstborns, only children, and perfectionism. Still ahead are Blended Family Birth Order 103 and 104, which are designed to help last borns, middle borns, and second born children learn how to live in a stepfamily without being stepped on.

NOTES

1. See Kevin Leman, *The Birth Order Book* (Old Tappan, NJ: Fleming H. Revell Co., 1985), 60; and, *Growing Up Firstborn* (New York: Dell Publishing, 1989), 85–86.

2. David Stoop, *Hope for the Perfectionist* (Nashville: Thomas Nelson, 1987), 34.

3. Stoop, 34–35.

4. Jane Goodsell, *Not a Good Word About Anybody* (New York: Ballantine Books, 1988), 45–46, 50.

5. Used by permission.

6. Fritz Ridenour, *Untying Your Knots* (Old Tappan, NJ: Fleming H. Revell, Power Books, 1988), 112.

7. Used by permission.

CHAPTER 4

Blended Family Birth Order 103

Why Last Borns Need Lots of Attention in the Stepfamily

As a psychologist who uses birth order as one of several counseling tools, I am always interested in what the skeptics have to say about it. For example, in an article appearing in *U.S. News and World Report,* the author observes that many researchers have backed away from using the "notion" of birth order as a way to characterize human personalities.

It is interesting, however, to note that this same article goes on to mention research done at MIT—a twenty-year analysis of four thousand scientists—that found those who were firstborn were much more conservative, much more competitive, and even less agreeable (due to their perfectionism, no doubt). *Later born* scientists, however, were consistently more open-minded and flexible, and therefore, they were the ones who led the way to radical scientific revolutions.[1]

Obviously, one piece of research doesn't prove anything, but what this study does suggest is that later born children grow up to be quite a bit different from firstborns or only children. And later borns play a major role in keeping the birth order blender whirring at "juicing" velocity.

Before we look at more blended family birth order collisions, let's see how much you know about the characteristics of those born later in the family. Here's a little pop quiz. Choose one answer only for each question.

1. *Who are the master negotiators and mediators?*
___*A. Firstborns*   ___*C. Middle borns*
___*B. Second borns*   ___*D. Last borns*

2. *Who are the best bets to stay married?*
___*A. Firstborns*   ___*C. Middle borns*
___*B. Second borns*   ___*D. Last borns*

3. *Who feels left out at home?*
___*A. Firstborns*   ___*C. Middle borns*
___*B. Second borns*   ___*D. Last borns*

4. *Whose birth order is hardest to spot?*
___*A. Firstborns*   ___*C. Middle borns*
___*B. Second borns*   ___*D. Last borns*

5. *Which birth order winds up most often on TV selling cars?*

___A. Firstborns   ___C. Middle borns
___B. Second borns   ___D. Last borns

6. Who is most likely to spoil the annual Christmas picture by goofing off?
___A. Firstborns   ___C. Middle borns
___B. Second borns   ___D. Last borns

7. Who usually has an "I'll show them" attitude?
___A. Firstborns   ___C. Middle borns
___B. Second borns   ___D. Last borns

8. Who loves to gain attention by being cute and entertaining?
___A. Firstborns   ___C. Middle borns
___B. Second borns   ___D. Last borns

9. Who is most likely to be the direct opposite of the sibling born just before?
___A. Firstborns   ___C. Middle borns
___B. Second borns   ___D. Last borns

10. Who is most likely to enjoy reading people rather than reading books?
___A. Firstborns   ___C. Middle borns
___B. Second borns   ___D. Last borns

The answer to questions 1 through 4 is middle children; the answer to questions 5 through 8 is last borns; questions 9 and 10: second borns.

Last Borns Demand and Usually Get Attention

At the bottom of the birth order ladder is the last born, also affectionately known as "the baby of the family." When two families blend and two last borns come together, there are usually sparks. Remember Tiffany, Phil's youngest child, and Tina, Peggy's last born? Tiffany and Tina were always getting into it for one reason or another, but the prime motivation behind their scraps was a constant battle to be in the limelight. Although Tiffany was four years older than Tina, she was still a "baby" in many ways, and she didn't like competition from a little twerp who suddenly could claim to be youngest in their blended family.

When we generalize about firstborns and onlies, we usually call them serious; but when we generalize about last borns, we come up with phrases like "charming little manipulators," "precocious," "engaging show-offs," "the comedians of the family who keep everyone in stitches." While there is no hard and fast rule about the birth order of comedians, it's interesting to note that Billy Crystal, Eddie Murphy, Goldie Hawn, and Charlie Chaplin are all the youngest of their sex in their families.

I'm Still Mugging for the Camera

I can speak with some authority on babies of the family because I was born third and last in the Leman family zoo, which included my sister, Sally, and right behind her, my brother, Jack. And I can say with certainty that babies of the family do like to show off, have fun, and make people laugh. I was all of that and more while growing up (and still am in many ways, for that matter).

Even my nickname—Cub—which I received when I was eleven days old, labeled me "the baby." As early as I can remember I was the cute little Cubby of my family, and though I had been born last, I always knew I was not least.

If there is anything that babies of the family like, it's attention, and I certainly vied for my share. I played the role of an affectionate, lovable Dennis the Menace to the hilt because I wanted one thing in life—to have people laugh, point, or comment about the Cub and his antics.

Several years ago, my family threw a surprise party for my fiftieth birthday. Among the many white elephant gifts I received was a note from my cousin Carol, which I'll always treasure. As she described the great times we spent together during summers when we were kids, she wrote:

There was always this little kid running around—my cousin Cubby. Never in one place for very long, his actions fluctuated between entertainment and harassment! He basked in the glorious commotion he created—his conversation, his movement, and that face. Eyes crossed, nose scrunched, and tongue wagging, he loved every minute of it.

Fifty years later, some things have changed—our summer gathering has moved . . . and we have grown quite a bit. But someone is still running around, never in one place for very long. Someone is still entertaining. Harassing? I'm not sure, but I would guess maybe just a little on special occasions. And that face, it hasn't changed one little bit!

Mom Prayed for a *C* on
My Report Card

The two good reasons that I behaved in such an attention-seeking manner weren't really my parents. They were my brother, Jack, who was five years older, captain of the football team, and an excellent student; and my sister, Sally, who was eight years older, captain of the cheerleaders and a *summa cum laude* in everything else.

With those two superstars above me, it was obvious that I had nowhere to go but into the entertainment field, so to speak. I certainly didn't get any attention with my grade point average, except sad shakes of my mom's head when I brought home my *D*s and *F*s. Poor Mom spent almost as much time at school as I did. At times she must have considered having her mail forwarded straight to the school because she was usually there looking into my latest escapade or trying to help the teachers discover how to motivate her baby Cub. I think my mother constantly prayed for just one *C* on my report card as a sign from the Almighty that there was, indeed, *something* between my ears after all.

In all candor, however, my mom was something of a pushover for a manipulator like me. I soon learned that I liked long weekends, and I often found a way to take off Fridays or Mondays—or both. Sometimes I just plain ditched school, but on many occasions I would "get sick," faking stomach pains or a headache. Although she was a registered nurse, my mother was a sucker for my "symptoms." She was sure they might lead to something serious, so of course, I had to stay home. Strangely enough, every day just before 3:00 P.M. when the kids got out of school, I would undergo a miraculous recovery, and infection would leave my body instantly.

Because of my *que sera sera* approach to school, I graduated fourth in my high school class (from the bottom). You may wonder how I got as high as fourth from the bottom. I had some interesting schoolmates, including one kid who made the same bookends four years in a row in wood shop.

Perhaps I always knew that I was destined for more than being the class clown and sitting in the principal's office. I can recall being in the lower reading group at age six, the crows, and watching some of my classmates—particularly the little girl who loved to eat paste—and thinking, *I know I don't really belong in this group!* Even way back then, I was well aware that I was destined for something besides underachievement, but it didn't happen until I reached young adulthood.

Actually, there was nothing wrong with my brain, only my attitude, which changed drastically after I got kicked out of one college and almost flunked out of another. At that point, I made some life-transforming decisions, and while my propensity for being a comedian and entertainer never faded, I did buckle down and eventually earned a doctorate. I often share my story when I speak, just to let despairing parents (and stepparents) know that kids who seem to be absolutely hopeless can turn around and head in the other direction. I am living proof that it does happen.

Peter Would Have Given Me a Run for My Money

One of the most manipulative last borns I'd ever seen in a blended family was little Peter, age five, who with his three older brothers and mother, Mary, blended with Fred, the father of three girls. Fred's daughters were in the custody of their mother, but every other weekend they would come for visits, and one month during the summer they were with Fred and Mary full-time.

The two biggest clues to why there could be problems in this family are the birth orders of Fred and Mary. As I talked with them, I learned that he was an autocratic, controlling firstborn. What Fred said always went, and he said it so often his first wife finally went and took their girls with her.

Mary, on the other hand, was a permissive last born who had spoiled her sons, much to her first husband's disgust. He had tried to exert some discipline in the home, but to little avail because Mary was always there to make excuses for her boys and protect them. Family discipline was one of several issues that split them apart and drove Mary deeper and deeper into her martyr's shell. When the divorce became final, Jeremy was eight; Brad, six; Mark, three; and Peter was only one.

For four years, Mary had lived as a single mom. Desperately wanting her sons' love and devotion, she continued to spoil them rotten, and the rottenest of them all was Peter. Naturally, Peter grew up having his own way in everything, and he became a master of the temper tantrum to get what he wanted. Peter constantly took advantage of his mother, but with her martyr's personality, she actually welcomed it in a way.

Peter loved to set up his three older brothers, especially seven-year-old Mark. In a family with several siblings, you will usually find the friction and fighting going on between those who are closest in age. Obviously for little Peter, the brother just older than him provided the likeliest (and safest) target. Of course, after Mark belted him one, Peter always enjoyed watching Mom lower the boom on him.

When permissive Mary and her boys moved in with Fred, the autocratic controller, you can imagine what happened. Although their birth orders, firstborn and last born, suggested that they could have a happy marriage (more on this in chapter 7), their radically different parenting styles led to all kinds of problems. When Fred tried to lay down the law and "get some order in the family," it was *déjà vu* for Mary. Once again she had chosen a strong powerful man who appealed to her as a husband but was a nightmare as a father. She leaped to the defense of all four of her kids, particularly Peter.

And what happened when Jami, Judy, and Becky arrived every other weekend and for that month during the summer? Was it the Brady Bunch plus one? A better analogy would be *Apocalypse Now*. As the diagram of this newly blended family shows, birth orders were bumping heads everywhere.

Fred (firstborn authoritarian controller)	Mary (last born permissive martyr)
Jami—11	Jeremy—12
Judy—9	Brad—10
Becky—6	Mark—7
	Peter—5

Naturally, Jami squared off with her stepbrother, Jeremy. Before her dad married "that woman with those four boys," there had been no doubt who was kingpin in her family. Whatever she and her sisters did, Jami was the boss and she called the shots. But after the blend, she had to contend with a (ugh!) boy one year older than she was and another (ugh!) boy a year younger. Now she was sandwiched between these cretins who challenged her at every turn.

Right below Jami was Judy, a nine year old who perfectly fit the description of middle child. And if it weren't tough enough to be a middle child between two sisters, in her blended family Judy had to look across the dinner table at two more middle children, Brad and Mark. This was just what she didn't need—double trouble.

Becky Was No Match for Peter the Powerful

We've already seen that Peter had plenty of rivalry going with his three older brothers, particularly Mark, just two years ahead of him. But when his mother married a man with three girls, he quickly brought his guns to bear on them as well, particularly Becky, who was only one year older and his natural rival for "baby of the family."

Peter and Becky squared off in all kinds of ways. But Becky, a baby princess herself who had always gotten away with murder—even around her authoritarian daddy—was no match for Peter, who had an almost diabolical ability to manipulate everyone and cause uproars everywhere he went.

Peter's tricks weren't very original, but he was a master of making devious little moves when his parents weren't looking—sticking out his tongue or kicking and poking under the table. And whenever any of the older kids, Fred's or Mary's, retaliated in some way, he howled in agony and ran to his mother, who automatically provided sanctuary and solace.

According to Fred, Peter had gotten so bold he had gone beyond the devious and hard-to-prove maneuvers and was openly doing things to drive everyone crazy. One of his favorite tricks was to find Judy's or Jami's homework and scribble on it in crayon. He also loved going into their rooms and messing things up. But when Judy and Jami complained to their dad and he tried to do something about it, Mary was always there to defend little Peter, explaining that nobody understood him and that he was only five years old—what did they expect?

By the time Fred and Mary talked to me, their marriage wasn't on the rocks, but it wasn't sailing on calm waters either. As they sat together in my office, I told them, "The first thing you've both got to realize is that there are seven of them and only two of you. Kids today are unionized. For a while, at least, you're going to have to be happy with small victories. Fred, as the perfectionist and controller in the family, there will be lots of times when you stand back and, as you see the big picture, it will threaten to blow you away. You are the kind of guy who likes everything all in a row—no surprises, nothing out of place. With seven kids—and especially four stepkids—hardly a day will go by when everything you so carefully plan won't fall apart at least a little. You may not like the idea, but your mission right now is survival."

(We'll get back to Fred and Mary when we look more closely at their marriage in chapter 7 and at what they needed to change in their parenting style in chapter 9.)

Last Borns Carry Plenty of Their Own Burdens

I can identify and even empathize with little Peter because I grew up manipulating and taking advantage of my parents, my teachers, and any other adults I could victimize. I had fun teasing my big sister, Sally, but the person I saved my best shots for was my older brother, Jack.

I always had to walk softly around Jack, who I often referred to as "God." Being the mischievous Cub of the family, I loved to set Jack up to get in trouble with Mom or Dad. He'd come home from school, and I'd say, "Oh, 'God's' home. Hi, 'God.' How did running the world go today?" Then I'd have to pay the price as he socked me on the arm so hard I thought it would fall off. But I would go wailing to Mom, and Jack would have to do time in his room or some other penance, much to my delight.

I'm sure Jack remembers the day a "just fooling around" wrestling match between my best friend, Moon-head, and me turned into a serious rumble. My dad caught Jack cheering Moonhead on as he was getting the best of the Cub. Dad reminded Jack in no uncertain terms that "you always stick up for family," and then he gave Jack a rap on the side of the head, just to be sure he got the point.

When Jack got belted, I had mixed feelings. I felt sorry for him because baby brothers look up to big brothers and there had been other times when Jack protected me from neighborhood bullies. But now, while I was wrestling somebody who was usually my friend, Jack had decided to turn on me, or so it seemed. Still smarting from being mauled by Moonhead, I also felt good when my dad let Jack know who was boss and what his responsibilities were.

Actually, the whole thing was a typical example of how parents tend to make the older kid responsible for the younger. When my dad whacked Jack, his firstborn son, he was reminding him to stick up for family, true, but he was also reminding Jack that he was supposed to take care of his little brother as well, because he was in charge and it was understood that he was responsible.

You'll also find that last borns can be rebellious, critical, temperamental, spoiled, impatient, and impetuous. I was all of those at different times, too, as I suffered the fate of all babies who are considered the smallest, weakest, and least experienced. Naturally, last borns are not taken very seriously because they're "not big enough to do anything," or at least not anything right. In short, babies have to live in "the shadow of those who were Born Before," as their older siblings tend to write them off more often than not.[2]

Remember what I said about everything a firstborn does being a "big deal"? For last borns, it's just the opposite. Their first steps, their first successful tying of shoelaces, their first *anything* is more likely to be met with polite yawns or comments like, "Oh, will you look at that! Little Thaddeus has learned to do a somersault. Remember when Timothy did that?"

Without realizing it, these parents have sent little Thaddeus a discouraging message: "Your older brother has already done what you think is so special."

I got enough of those messages myself to develop my own rebellious streak. Mixed in with my last born charm and precociousness was the vow, "I'll show them!" That's part of the reason that I was willing to risk life and limb to goad Jack into a murderous rage. I not only wanted to set him up; I wanted to show him I was someone to be reckoned with.

Besides "I'll show them," there are many other typical last born phrases, many of which I uttered while growing up:

- "I did it just for laughs."

- "Won't you help me?"

- "I was just kidding."

- "Why don't you believe me?"

- "Why do they always get to do that?"

- "I never get to do anything!"

- "That's not fair!"

- "Why can't I go?"

Last borns often come across like absentminded space cadets who walk around with their fly unzipped, their underwear in their back pocket, or some crucially obvious buttons unbuttoned. But they aren't as helpless and incompetent as their older siblings may think. Babies of the family are often perceptive people persons who go into professions like counseling, teaching, and sales.

Helpful Questions for Last Born Stepparents

If you are the baby of your family and today are a parent yourself—and a stepparent to boot—here are some questions to consider:

1. *Are you a good role model?* Before demanding that your spouse and stepchildren act more responsibly, check how well you are doing as a responsible adult. Babies of the family are notorious for their irresponsibility, and maybe you are acting irresponsibly and not even realizing it. Ask yourself: "On a scale of 1 to 10, how responsible a role model am I for my family?" If you rated yourself below 5, you've identified an important area to work on.

2. *Are you messy or are you a neatfreak?* Many last

Positive and Negative Aspects of Being a Last Born

Last Born Trait	Positive Aspect	Negative Aspect
Charming	Likeable, fun to be around	Manipulative, maybe a little flaky
People oriented	Relates well to others	Lacking in discipline, would rather talk than work
Affectionate	Caring and lovable, wants to help	Can be gullible, easily taken advantage of
Uncomplicated	What you see is what you get, seldom uptight	Can be absentminded or seem like an airhead
Seeks attention	Entertaining and funny	Can be temperamental, spoiled, or impatient
Tenacious, persistent	Won't take no for an answer	Can paint himself into a corner, sees things only "my way."

borns are messies. If you fall anywhere in that category, be slow to demand neatness from your stepkids when you won't be neat yourself.

3. *Are you self-centered or others-centered?* Because they're often spoiled, last borns are typically self-centered. As an adult, you have probably learned to cover up your self-centeredness quite well, but the pressures of being a stepparent may bring it to the surface. For one thing, stepparents don't get a lot of thanks, credit, or kudos. If this is true of your lot as a stepparent, maybe you're getting upset partly because of your last born self-centeredness. As a baby of the family myself, I know whereof I speak; it's easy for a last born to throw self-pity parties. When you feel one coming on, remind yourself of Dr. Leman's First Rule of the Family: No one person is more important than the entire group.

4. *How likely are you to blame others for your mistakes?* Refusing to accept blame is another classic last born trait, and if you're doing this in a stepfamily, you can get stepped on—and fast! If nothing else, you'll be stepping on others and causing bruised feelings where there are already many emotional wounds.

5. *Are you used to the limelight?* Are you the funny, gifted, charming one? If the rest of your family could be honest, what would they say about your interest in them? Do you ask them about their ideas, their schedules, and what they think, or are you usually talking more about yourself and your plans?

6. *Do you use your gifts and skills positively?* If you're a typical last born, you have abilities that can be of great use in a blended family. For example, you may be gifted in sizing up relationships and lightening up tense situations with a little laid-back humor. You probably feel comfortable in social situations, and you like to

solve problems with the aid of others. And you're also good at getting others to do things you'd like to have accomplished. Last borns are skilled at management from the bottom, meaning that you baby princes and baby princesses are able to persuade (and even manipulate a little bit) your way through situations that might stop others in their tracks.

Sally Didn't Let the Cub Slip Through the Cracks

As last borns grow up in their natural nuclear family, they are influenced deeply by older siblings for good and sometimes for not so good. By the time a last born is five or six, the grain of his wood is set (just as it is with any birth order). The typical last born needs, craves, and demands attention, and she gets it one way or another, sometimes by being cute and precocious, sometimes by being a little pest, or even sometimes by being a spoiled brat.

In chapter 9, we'll be looking at specific techniques for parenting last borns in a blended family. For now, however, keep one thing in mind: When death or divorce smashes his little world into smithereens, the last born can be a bundle of shattered nerves or an "I'll show them" time bomb ready to explode. Blended families need to make sure that last borns don't slip through the cracks, especially if a last born from one side of the blended family is suddenly shouldered out of the limelight by someone younger and cuter from the other side.

Burdened with their parenting load, parents of later borns may turn them over to their older brothers and sisters for instruction in some of the basics of life. I've already mentioned how my older brother, Jack, was held accountable for "protecting me" from neighborhood bullies and such, but the person who really moved in to care for me was my big sister, Sally.

Sally was always a protective, nurturing mother figure to me, despite all of the trouble I caused her with my teasing and other antics. I still remember the time she took me shopping. I must have been around seven or eight while she was fifteen or sixteen and "really grown up" in my eyes. We stopped to eat in an old-fashioned luncheonette, and as I looked at the menu I saw the words *turkey sandwich* in print for the first time in my life. All I could think of was how much I loved turkey and how good that sandwich would taste. Then, at the end of the line came the bad news . . . eighty cents!

This was high-class territory, over three times what my usual hamburger would have cost. Just then Sally asked, "What would you like for lunch?"

I must have looked rather wistful as I said, "Could I have a turkey sandwich?"

"Oh, sure," Sally said, and she dug in her purse to find the money she had earned the hard way—baby-sitting someone besides me. All I could think of as I munched my turkey sandwich was, *Isn't this neat, my big sis bought me a turkey sandwich!*

When I think of who I am as a person, the two key people I focus on are my mom and Sally. I saw little of my dad while I was growing up. He would usually not get home until eight o'clock at night, when I was either already in bed or headed that way in a few minutes. I got to know Dad much better as an adult, and we had some great times together before he died. But when I was the little last born tearing around the house to see what kind of mischief—and worse—I could get into, I could have easily slipped through the cracks. I could have been written off as somebody too little to matter that much, except for being an occasional pain in the neck. Sally went out of her way to make me feel important. She taught me that I could contribute to the family and that I could even have responsibilities. And when my clowning and antics went past the line of good taste into bad behavior, she was still patient and longsuffering (although there were probably a few times when she had fleeting thoughts about reducing the cub population by one).

As you look around your blended family, you may see someone slipping through the cracks. It could easily be a baby, or it could be someone else. It could be your natural child or your stepchild. Whoever it is, try to be to that little life what my sister, Sally, was to me. In the end, it will be worth all the effort.

NOTES

1. Erica Goode, "The Secret World of Siblings," *U.S. News and World Report,* Jan. 10, 1994, 48.

2. Mopsy Strange Kennedy, "A Last-Born Speaks Out—At Last," *Newsweek,* Nov. 7, 1977, 22.

CHAPTER 5

Blended Family Birth Order 104

How Middles Seek Respect in the Stepfamily

If you're a middle child, you've probably been reading all this birth order stuff and muttering, "When is he going to get to *me?*" It's typical for middle children to feel left out and ignored. After *The Birth Order Book* was published, I'd often get letters from middle borns saying something like this:

Dear Dr. Leman:

I counted the number of pages in The Birth Order Book *and fewer are devoted to middle children than any other birth order! What gives?*

Feeling ignored,

A Middle Child Reader

My response to these middle children who think they were given short shrift in *The Birth Order Book* is always the same:

Dear Middle Child:

So what? What's the big deal? Besides, you're used to it!

Love,

Dr. Leman

Actually, it's true that the middle child gets fewer pages in *The Birth Order Book* (ten compared to fourteen for last borns and twelve for firstborns). One reason for this difference is that middle children are the hardest to define, describe, or generalize about in a meaningful way.[1]

A major problem anyone faces in defining a "typical" middle born is that he can be in any number of positions in the family: second of three, third of four, fourth of five, and so on. As I said in *The Birth Order Book,* the *branching off effect* is a critical factor when dealing with a middle child. By *branching off* I mean that as each child is born into the family, he usually plays off the child just older and develops a different approach to operating in life, a different "specialty" that is personal and individual.

For example, if a firstborn is the family bookworm or scholar, the second born might well be the family athlete or musician. Naturally, some genetically inherited skills are necessary for such pursuits, but as a rule each child wants to carve out his own niche and therefore branches off in a somewhat different direction than the sibling just older.

This branching off effect is the reason it's so hard to develop a definite and consistent list of characteristics for middle children. As you will quickly see, the following descriptions seem to cancel each other out, but all of these characteristics are possibilities for middle children because so much depends on how they bounce off their older brothers or sisters.

The Middle Born: Inconsistent Paradox

Sociable, friendly, outgoing
Takes life in stride, laidback
Easygoing, not competitive
Peacemaker, mediator

Excellent negotiator
Impatient, easily frustrated
Quiet, shy
Rebel, family goat
Avoids conflict

Zack Became a Middle Child—or Did He?

A good example of how different middle child traits can bounce off each other in a blended family was the remarriage of George and Dorene, both middle children themselves. George was a sociable, friendly, outgoing middle child, a good peacemaker and mediator. Dorene, a quiet and shy middle child, tried to avoid conflict whenever possible.

When Dorene married her first husband, Robert, all her friends said he wasn't right for her. She married him anyway because he was ten years older and seemed to be the father she never had. The marriage lasted seven years and produced one child, Zack. When Zack had just turned six, Robert decided he had had enough of being tied down and left with no forwarding address.

With the help of her parents, Dorene managed to find a job, and she scraped by as a single mom. When she met George about a year later, she could immediately see that he was everything Robert was not. George had also been married before, and he had custody of his teenage son, Tommy. His first wife, Josie, had custody of their other two children, Timmy and Jane, but George could see them on Wednesdays and every other weekend.

As Dorene watched George interact with his children, she quickly saw that he could be the father that Zack had always needed. Dorene and George dated for a year and a half before getting married and bringing together the following blend:

Dorene (nonconfrontive middle child)	George (peacemaking middle child)
Zack—9	Tommy—13
	Timmy—10
	Jane—7

The question for Dorene now is, where is Zack in the birth order blender now that she has married George? Throughout the week, when it's just Zack and Tommy, is Zack, four years younger than Tommy, the "last born" in the family? And on weekends when Timmy and Jane arrive, where does Zack fit in? Because Jane is younger and Timmy is one year older, does Zack become a middle child?

When I counseled with Dorene, who talked to me first, she was worried about Zack and how he was blending with George's children. Zack and Tommy squabbled a lot; and when Timmy and Jane came, Tommy joined forces with them to make Zack feel unimportant or worse.

"After Jane and Timmy leave, it takes at least a couple of days to get Zack out of his shell," Dorene complained.

"Tommy's behavior isn't too hard to explain," I said.

"For blended family kids, blood ties are always stronger than their parents' wedding vows. Remember, Tommy, Timmy, and Jane are siblings, and when they get together, Zack is the outsider. Who does Zack have the most trouble with?" I asked.

"It's about even," Dorene replied. "Zack is just about Timmy's size, and he competes with him whenever he can. And he likes to boss Jane around because she's younger."

"Again, it's not too hard to understand what's going on with Zack. While being in the blended family may place him in the role of baby or second child with Tommy and in the role of middle child when the other two kids arrive, he was an *only* child for a long time—he never had any competition. He used to rule the roost and is accustomed to getting his way, not having to share. That's why he squabbles with Tommy so much. But when he has to cope with all three of George's kids, it's more than he can handle and he goes into his shell. He doesn't want to have to deal with all this."

"I never thought of it quite like that," Dorene replied. "But all of this just says to me that if we could have all of George's kids with us all the time we could probably blend everybody together a lot more easily. With Timmy and Jane coming and going, it's a constant disruption."

As I talked with Dorene, I learned that in her typical nonconfrontive style she didn't share a lot of her concerns with her husband. George was oblivious to the whole problem, not noticing (or choosing to ignore) the subtle and not so subtle jabs at Zack by the Tommy/Timmy/Jane alliance on weekends.

Fortunately, I was able to talk with George when he accompanied Dorene on a second visit to my office. The consummate middle child peacemaker and mediator,

George was not belligerent or insensitive, just unaware. I urged both of them to start exchanging ideas about what they could do to build up Zack's self-esteem. Dorene also needed to think about her role as stepmother. She had deliberately chosen to have only one child, and now she was the full-time mother of two children, with two more kids coming every other weekend and Wednesdays.

What Middles Have in Common with Rodney Dangerfield

What can we say, then, that is typical about the middle child? Actually, there are several things, and I've already illustrated one: middle children just don't feel they get a whole lot of respect or notice, not even in books on birth order! Middle children are, in effect, the Rodney Dangerfields of this world—they "don't get no respect!" The key reason that they feel so disrespected is that they feel squeezed between older and younger siblings.

Middle born children will tell you that they usually didn't feel all that special while growing up. The firstborn had his spot—carrier of the family banner and responsible for everything. The last born had his comfy little role, but the middle born had no distinctive place to call his own.

This was the case with Timmy, George's middle child, who had felt squeezed for the first nine years of his life. When his father divorced his mother and then his older brother went to live with his dad, Timmy was left to be top dog in his household. In many ways he became the firstborn of his family, getting privileges and responsibilities that would normally have gone to his older brother had he been living with their mother. When Timmy had to go to his dad's for the weekend, all that changed, and he was back to his middle child role, which he disliked intensely. This was one reason why he liked to pick on the nearest safe target, who, of course, was Zack.

Middle borns just seem to be easily overlooked, and maybe that's why there are so few pictures of them in the family photo album. There may be hundreds, seemingly thousands, of pictures of the firstborn. And the baby of the family will make sure she attracts enough attention to fill a few album pages. For some strange reason, however, which I have confirmed by polling middle born children around the world, there are seldom many pictures of the middle child, and what photos there are have him included with the others—squeezed again between the older sibling and the younger sibling.

Another thing that can be said of many middle born children is that they typically place great importance on their peer group. The middle child is well-known for going outside the home to make friends faster than anybody else in the family. When a child feels like a fifth wheel at home, friends become very important; as a result, many middle children (but not all, of course) tend to be the social lions of the family. While firstborns, typically, have fewer friends, middle children often have many.

Middle children have a propensity to leave home first and live farther from the family than anyone else. I observed a dramatic illustration of this tendency while I was a guest on Oprah Winfrey's show. The subject that day was sibling rivalry. Three charming young women, all sisters, were among the guests, and we quickly learned that the firstborn and the last born were residents of the Eastern state where they had grown up. They had settled down near their parents and other family members. But the middle child had moved to the West Coast.

I suppose she could have gotten another two thousand miles farther away by moving to Hawaii, but her point was still well made. Middle children are the ones who will most often physically distance themselves from the rest of the family. It's not necessarily because they're on the outs with everyone else. They simply like to do their own thing, make their own friends, and live their own lives.

Middles Are Often Good Team Players

Because he feels like an outsider in his own family, the middle child often becomes a free spirit in many ways. He may be the one to reject the family values and accept his peer group's values instead. He may find his sense of connection by being part of a team (middle children are known as good team players), a club, or a gang. Whatever the group might be, the middle child sees that group as his—a second family, so to speak. No wonder he spends so much time with them. His family can't squeeze him or neglect him when he is with his other "family" on another turf.

All of this is not to say that middle children totally ignore their siblings or the rest of the family. One common characteristic of the middle child is that she is a good mediator or negotiator. She comes naturally into this role because she's often right in the middle, between big brother and little sister, whatever the case may be. And because she can't have Mom and Dad all to herself, she learns the fine art of compromise. Obviously, these skills are assets in adult life, and middle children often become the best adjusted adults in the family.

Let's take time out right here for a quickie quiz: Name one or more recent presidents of the United States who were considered skilled in foreign affairs and diplomacy.

If you guessed Richard Nixon or George Herbert Walker Bush, most political observers would say you're right. I just want to add that both men were middle children.

So, while middle children are harder to define, they do have some identifying characteristics. And, like other birth orders, the middle child may give you clues to his identity with typical expressions that he uses on a day-to-day basis:

- "Nobody pays attention to me."

- "I don't get much respect."

- "Could I go first for a change?"

At the same time, as he develops his negotiating and mediating skills, the middle child also says:

- "Let's try to work it out."

- "What do you think?"

- "It doesn't matter."

- "It's no big deal."

Squeezed, ignored, shown little respect, an outsider who barely makes it into the family photo album—all this makes it sound as if the middle child is doomed to unhappiness, but not so. Like Johnny Cash's "Boy

Named Sue," the middle child learns to be tough and resilient and becomes on average the most well-adjusted adult among all birth orders. Hence, middle children bring valuable skills and qualities to the blended family, especially the ability to negotiate and mediate.

If you're a stepparent wondering who to enlist as an ally among your stepchildren, you might look to the middle child. At the same time, keep in mind that the middle born children in your blended family are the most secretive and the most prone to embarrassment. Play your cards right with the middle child, don't come on too strong or too fast, and you may wind up with a very good friend.

That was my advice to Dorene in regard to her stepson, Timmy, the middle child who was giving her son, Zack, a bad time. With my coaching (remember, Dorene is a nonconfrontive middle child), she got bold enough to sit down alone with Timmy one weekend and asked him point blank why he disliked Zack so much.

"Because he tries to be bossy, and I'm older than he is!" Timmy shot back.

"I know Zack tries to get bossy," Dorene said softly, "but let me try to explain what it was like for him growing up an only child. He didn't have any brothers or sisters, so he never learned to share a whole lot. When he went to preschool, he was the biggest and most capable kid there. He could read, play ball—do practically anything—ahead of anyone else. You see him as someone who's younger than you are, a pain in the neck, but Zack sees himself as king of the hill. When you and Tommy and Jane gang up on him, it wipes him out. What he really wants is your friendship, but he feels like an outsider when you're here."

I also encouraged Dorene to talk to Zack and let him

Positive and Negative Aspects of Being a Middle Born

Middle Born Trait	Positive Aspect	Negative Aspect
Feels squeezed and rootless	Learns not to be spoiled	May be rebellious because he feels he doesn't fit
Sociable	Makes friends easily	May make the wrong kind of friends or place too much importance on sociable activity
Compromising	Easy to get along with	Can be taken advantage of
Compatible	Willing to work things out	May not share real feelings
Mediator	Good negotiator and peacemaker	May be willing to have peace at any price
Independent	Entrepreneurial, willing to take risks	Uncooperative, bullheaded or stubborn

know that although he had been an only child until he was nine, that was no longer the case, and he had to learn to share and cooperate with the other people who are now a part of his family. Dorene reported to me later that the boys had made a little progress in being friendly toward each other, and she and George were vigilant on weekends to be sure that his three didn't have as many opportunities to shut Zack out or gang up on him.

Why Middle Children Make Good Stepparents

If you're a typical middle child, you have learned skills in negotiating and compromising that should give you an edge in building your blended family. Keep the following tips in mind:

1. *Remember how it feels to get unfair treatment.* You probably know quite a bit about being left out, ignored, or given little or no respect. Be aware that your stepchildren probably have been feeling the same way, regardless of their particular birth order. Do all you can to include your stepchildren, pay attention to them, and show them respect, even though they probably won't do the same for you. You won't mind—you're used to it, remember?

The trick, of course, is to not neglect your own children while trying to reach out to your stepchildren. This was Dorene's fear, especially since Zack was being ganged up on by Tommy, Timmy, and Jane.

2. *Remember how it feels to be easily embarrassed.* You may still be prone to embarrassment, even if you don't admit it. From your leadership position as an adult, do all you can to keep from embarrassing others in the family, particularly your stepchildren. If something

embarrassing happens to a stepchild, move in with as much empathy and T.L.C. as you will be allowed to give.

When I talked with George, I learned that he had often been embarrassed as a kid, so I urged him to do everything he could on weekends to help Zack out of embarrassing situations when his kids ganged up on his stepson.

3. *Avoid playing comparison games.* Avoid them like the plague. All your life you have known what it feels like to be compared to older and younger siblings in any number of areas. Be especially careful not to compare your children to your spouse's children. Accept everyone where he or she is at the moment in this blender called a stepfamily and work from there. This advice suited the nonconfrontive Dorene to a tee. As she worked at refusing to compare Zack to her three stepchildren, and, vice versa, it made a real difference in the way the kids got along.

"I know it's hard to see your husband's three kids giving Zack a hard time," I told her, "but as you look at your three stepkids, remember all of the anger and pain they bring with them into your blended family. Tommy is living with you now because he took an emotional beating from his mom until she couldn't 'handle him' anymore. Naturally, he's going to find it hard to approach you, the new female authority figure in his life. As for the other two, every time they come over on weekends, they are reminded that their dad is no longer with their mom and is married to another woman."

As Dorene realized that she was the adult who needed to help her stepchildren, not just dislike them for being unfriendly toward her own child, she was able to deal more effectively with the conflict situations that continued to come up. Instead of wondering why George's children couldn't be as "nice and kind" as her own son, she took a more objective view and realized that at times Zack was setting up the other kids to make it look as if they were ganging up on him when they really weren't.

(You'll read more in chapter 9 about how to avoid the trap of playing favorites as you deal with the problem of stepsibling rivalry.)

4. *If you're a "free spirit" middle child, don't despair.* Your blended family may be fencing you in, but duty comes ahead of desire. At least you can empathize with family members who like to do their own thing, too! On many days, that category seems to include all the kids, yours and his. Stepparents can't always indulge themselves in doing their own thing as much as they would like. When you feel an independent streak coming on, remind yourself of the first law of the family, which bears repeating often: "No one person is more important than the whole group."

What About the Two-Child Family?

One birth order combination that we haven't looked at yet is the two-child family. Here there is no middle child, but second borns will certainly have one characteristic in common with any later born child: they will size up their firstborn siblings and decide how they will branch off.

All this sizing up goes on very early—in infancy and up through age five or six—while the child is forming what I call a *life-style*—an individual way of perceiving life and deciding how to meet personal goals. We'll look more closely at life-style in chapter 6. And as the second born looks up at the firstborn, he may decide not to branch off as much as to compete. His goal: to knock the firstborn off his pedestal. Counselors call this phenomenon *dethronement.*

Actually, all firstborns experience a certain degree of dethronement the minute a little brother or sister is born. Up until that moment, they have been absolutely number one and the apple of everyone's eye. All of a sudden, there is another little apple on the limb, and the firstborn is no longer special. In fact, if parents aren't careful, their firstborn can suffer serious self-esteem problems due to dethronement.

Smart parents go out of their way to let the firstborn know, even before little second born comes home from the hospital, that he (the firstborn) is very special and a whole lot bigger and more capable than the little baby "who can't do anything yet." Single parents who remarry need to be extra aware of the dethronement factor if they have a child in the new marriage.

Even when a firstborn is well prepared for the arrival of a little brother or sister, even when she appears to welcome the second born, do not be fooled. There is an automatic rivalry that exists between the siblings. As the new little arrival looks things over from inside the crib, he decides if he can go for it and confront the firstborn on a head-to-head basis. When a second born child goes one-on-one with his firstborn sibling and actually takes over the leadership or achievement role commonly reserved for the oldest child, it's called *role reversal.* As far as family roles are concerned, the second born can become the firstborn of the family.

Firstborn-Second Born Rivalry at the Leman House

Sande and I have watched with interest the rivalry between our firstborn, Holly, and her second born sister,

Krissy, which began approximately two hours after Krissy came home from the hospital. We still have the home movie that shows all four of us posed for a family portrait when Holly was about two and a half and Krissy was around a year old. The first few times we watched the movie, we really didn't see what was going on, but finally Sande pointed out, "Look! Holly is elbowing Krissy in the head!"

As the girls grew older, the rivalry increased, but to be honest, it was kept alive more by Holly than by Krissy, who was quite content in her second born role; however, she'd never back away from a challenge. A competitive exacting firstborn to the teeth, Holly was always wanting to race Krissy on land or sea (our backyard pool). She also loved to compete with Krissy in singing contests the two girls usually held in the back seat of our car as we drove somewhere.

Sande and I were often called upon to be judges during these Star Search sessions, which really weren't much of a contest. Second born Krissy could sing like a little bird, but firstborn Holly, who was practically tone-deaf, sounded like Drāno. After giving Krissy three straight decisions, we'd sometimes let up and say, "Okay, Holly, you won that one." I'd look in the rearview mirror and see the most astounded look on Krissy's face. She wondered if her parents had gone tone-deaf, too!

This past Christmas when our girls were home from college for the holidays, we could see that the rivalry was still there. One of our son's school books was lying out on the hall table encased in the typical school book cover, which had many inviting places on which to write. Krissy had dropped by and written, "Hi, Kev. I love you. Your big sister, Krissy."

And right next to it was a similar note from Holly,

who had apparently come by a little later and written, "Hi, Kev. I love you, too, besides *I'm nicer!*"

For years Holly has tried to run Krissy's life, and we've had to tell her over and over, "Holly, paddle your *own* canoe!" Last Christmas we all had a great time listening to some tapes made almost twenty years ago at Grandma's house, and we could clearly hear Holly's little voice saying, "Krissy, you don't want that—give *me* that." We all had a good laugh, including Holly, who was good-natured about it because overall she and her sister are very fond of each other and get along very well now.

A major factor in the amount of rivalry that develops between first and second born children is their sex. As Holly and Krissy illustrate, when you have firstborn and second born girls, there is bound to be fairly keen rivalry. Obviously, the same holds true for firstborn and second born boys, usually to an even greater degree. When, however, you have a firstborn boy and second born girl, or vice versa, the rivalry is usually tempered quite a bit. Instead of going head-to-head, they tend to go their own way and carve out their own turf, where they each operate quite happily.

This is what happened with my older sister, Sally, and my older brother, Jack. Sally was the superior student, but not by much. Sally captained the cheerleaders while Jack captained the football team. They went their separate successful ways.

Whatever the combination in a two-child family, it is obvious that there is no middle child. If the first and second born are only a few years apart, the firstborn will probably develop typical firstborn characteristics, and the second born will go more in the direction of being the baby of the family (unless, of course, the second born overtakes the firstborn and effects a role reversal).

Bryant Gumbel Fooled Me Completely

Role reversals are something I usually put in the category I call birth order variables, which can almost always account for why a person doesn't act at all like the typical descriptions of his birth order (see chapter 2). We usually don't see role reversals between first and second born siblings who are more than two years apart, but every now and then there is an exception.

One of the most striking examples of how even I can be fooled happened when I was on the "Today Show," cohosted by Bryant Gumbel and Katie Couric. Katie was slated to interview me that morning on birth order, and before the show started, we had chatted backstage and I had casually mentioned that she seemed to be the youngest of her family. Later, while we were on the air, Katie asked, "How did you know I was the youngest? That's amazing to me, how did you know that?"

"Well . . . you're very engaging and seem affectionate, really come across fun-loving, and my guess would be that you have a sister or sisters, but I wouldn't be surprised to find a brother or a wonderful relationship with your father."

Katie looked at me with still more amazement. "I have two sisters and a brother. You're clairvoyant, Dr. Leman." A few seconds later as the interview ended, Katie was still smiling and shaking her head.

But it's a good thing that Bryant Gumbel hadn't interviewed me that day. I would have bet my birth order credentials on Bryant being a firstborn. Impeccably dressed, suavely aggressive, a perfectionist of the first order in all that he does, Bryant Gumbel would be taken for a firstborn or only child by any birth order specialist. It turns out, however, that Bryant is the second born in his family. His older brother, Greg, has also made his mark in the broadcasting field as a sportscaster on ESPN and CBS, including anchoring the 1994 Winter Olympic Games.

I have never had the opportunity to chat with either of the Gumbel brothers to try to find out what happened. Was there some kind of role reversal? Possibly, but one thing is for sure: Bryant, three years younger than his big brother, must have had the constitution of a salmon to leap over many an obstacle as he carved out a piece of turf for himself that is normally reserved strictly for firstborns.

Over the years I've often been put on the spot by talk show hosts or other interviewers who want me to guess their birth order, or perhaps the birth order of our waitress, or whoever else might be handy. My batting average has always been .900 or better, but every now and then a Bryant Gumbel will remind me that there is nothing about birth order that is set in concrete.

As I mentioned earlier, variables can have a powerful influence on how children of different birth orders turn out. In chapter 2, for example, we saw how the variable of *sex* created six firstborns in Phil and Peggy's family.

Another important variable is *spacing* (the number of years between each child). Suppose a family has a firstborn girl followed by another girl, just a year or so later. Then five years go by and a boy is born, followed by another boy two years after that. There are four children, but do we have a firstborn, two middles, and a baby? Probably not. Whenever there is a gap of five or more years, it usually means a second "family" has begun. So what you have is a firstborn girl and a second born girl in one family, and a firstborn boy and a second born boy in the other.

Another family has a firstborn boy followed by a second born girl just three years later. Then there is a gap of ten years and another girl is born. Is the last born strictly a baby of the family? It is more likely that she would grow up with many only child characteristics because her much older brother and sister would be more like an aunt and uncle to her than siblings. Again, you would have two "families"; one with a firstborn boy and a firstborn girl, the other with an only child.

One other powerful variable that needs to be mentioned is *physical differences*. For example, suppose a family has a firstborn boy who is rather short and slight. Three years later along comes his "little" brother, who quickly passes him in size, and as they go through their grade school years, the older boy has to look up to his younger brother, who is three inches taller and thirty pounds heavier.

Now, throw in the possibility that little brother is not only a lot bigger physically but is also a lot smarter and gets better grades in school. What you have in the making here is a role reversal where the second born actually assumes the firstborn privileges and responsibilities. I have seen it happen many times.

Or suppose a family has a boy followed two years later by another boy who has a congenital birth defect and can only get around with crutches. Two years later along comes a baby sister, who you can see would be a very special one in the family. But what about that special boy with the birth defect? Would there be a lot of pressure on him? No, the most pressure would be on his older brother who would get a lot of assignments to take care of his brother, as well as his baby sister.

Birth order puts you in your own corner of the family zoo, so to speak. But how you interact with the rest of the zoo is your own private journey to becoming the person you are today.

How Do Birth Orders Collide in Your Family?

The examples of birth order collisions in this chapter, as well as in chapter 2, only scratch the surface in showing how birth orders can bounce into and off of each other in a blended family. Take some time right now to diagram your own family's situation. If possible, ask your spouse to do the same. You may feel you already know where the pressure points are, but you will be surprised how helpful it is to put it on paper and discuss your perceptions with those of your spouse.

My birth order: _____ Spouse's birth order: _____

Firstborn: _____ Age __ Firstborn: _____ Age __

Second born: ____ Age __ Second born: ____ Age __

Third born: _____ Age __ Third born: _____ Age __

Fourth born: ____ Age __ Fourth born: ____ Age __

(Add additional information as needed. Be sure to stipulate who your last born child is.)

Circle the persons in each column who may be colliding with someone in the other column and draw a line between them. Then insert their names below and list specifics concerning how their birth orders collide.

Our major birth order collision is between: _____

_____

Our secondary birth order collision involves: _____

_____

Additional birth order collisions: _____

_____

When you are finished and your spouse is finished, compare notes to see if your perceptions are the same, then talk about what you can do to relieve birth order collision problems in your family. If you don't come up with a lot of ideas at the moment, don't be discouraged. Keep reading, especially in Part 3 of this book, where I discuss setting up a strategy for dealing with the birth order blender.

Life-style: A Major Cause of Birth Order Collisions

Birth order sets the stage for how each child develops what we call a *life-style*—that is, a unique way of living and interacting with others.

While still in the cradle, a child sizes up the world around her and decides what kind of a person she will be. Personalities are as varied as people. The reason for this variety is that all of us develop our own life theme, a certain personal motto that we adopt early in life. Everyone's life theme begins with the words, "I only count when . . ." How you finish that sentence determines your individual personality and how you will interact with others.

In an original nuclear family, it is difficult enough to deal with all the birth orders, life-styles, and life themes.

But when families blend and become binuclear, the life-style/birth order demolition derby begins in earnest. In the next chapter we'll see some examples of how this works out in daily family living, and you will also have the opportunity to assess your own life-style and life theme, as well as those of your spouse and children.

NOTE

1. See, for example, Bradford Wilson and George Edington, *First Child, Second Child* (New York: McGraw-Hill Book Co., 1981), 92.

CHAPTER 6

In This Blended Family, I Only Count When . . .

"I'm going crazy, Dr. Leman. It was hard enough keeping my own three kids happy before I got remarried, but when we moved in with Jim and his two, it got crazy. My older daughter, Taylor, has always had her feelings easily hurt. She constantly squabbles with her younger sister, Allison, who doesn't seem to care what people say. But they agree on one thing—their little brother, Tyler, is a twerp and they want to kill him most of the time."

Rebecca, thirty-seven and married a second time to Jim, had come to see me after sixteen months of having little success in her blended family.

"So far you've described your own kids—what's happened since you've blended with his kids?" I wondered.

"Sibling rivalry has turned into stepsibling war," she answered. "Taylor is the same age as Jim's older daughter, Roxanne, who is very pretty and knows it. She's constantly flaunting her looks and asking Taylor why she doesn't have any dates. And her younger brother, Rick, is just as bad. He's a star athlete, and he's always playing something. My son, Tyler, really admires Rick, but Rick won't give him the time of day—he calls him names and tells him to bug off. This makes Tyler mad, and he's always getting in Rick's things and causing problems. Dr. Leman, the house is a zoo. The other day Taylor screamed that she was sick of our family and was going to leave. Roxanne just laughed and told her she'd help her pack. What am I supposed to do?"

What's going on in Rebecca's family? Obviously, birth orders are colliding all over the place, but other powerful forces are at work as well. Everyone in any blended family brings two critical components to the mix:

- A *personal life-style*—a unique way of looking at oneself, other people, and the world. Every person sees life differently. For each of us, reality is what we see from behind our own eyes.

- A *life theme*—or personal motto, so to speak, which is lived out every day—actually every moment. We may seldom state our life theme in so many words, but it is there, directing our every move.

Life-style is a term coined by Alfred Adler, who founded the school of Individual Psychology in the early 1900s. Adler believed that from early infancy all of us start forming an individual life plan that causes us to pursue certain life goals. According to Adler, we would not know what to do with ourselves if we were not oriented to some goal or objective. As he put it, "We cannot think, feel, will, or act without the perception of some goal."[1]

Adler believed that when a baby is born he quickly sizes up what is going on around him (his environment) and starts forming his goals. Obviously, he doesn't do this consciously, making notes in his appointment book, but the information is all being registered in his little brain, nonetheless. Adler wrote:

> The goal of each human being is probably formed in the first months of his life. Even at this time, certain sensations play a role which evoke a response of joy or comfort in this child. Here the first traces of a philosophy of life come to the surface, although expressed in the most primitive fashion.[2]

You might be wondering where genetics come in. Does a child learn *everything* from her environment?

Good question. Psychologists have long argued over what influences a human being the most—heredity or environment. According to Rudolph Dreikurs, one of Alfred Adler's leading disciples, a growing child experiences both heredity and environment and draws his own conclusions. As he experiences his environment (mainly his family), he discovers where he is skilled and strong and where he is weak and lacking in ability. As the child sorts out all of his experiences, with their pluses and minuses, his personality takes shape.[3]

As an infant grows and pursues his primitive goals, he starts developing what Adler called a *style of life—life-style,* for short. Don't confuse Adler's use of the word *life-style* with what you read in today's magazines or newspapers. Adler wasn't talking about living on a certain income, driving a certain car, or wearing certain clothes.

What Adler meant by life-style was *how each of us functions psychologically to reach our goals*. Granted, we may not be able to spell out our goals, particularly when we're very young, but they are there, nonetheless, and they are controlling the way we perceive our world and the way we interact with those around us.

Every child is born with the need for attention, and one of his primary goals is to gain attention in one way or another. When a child's attempt to gain attention, either positively or negatively, doesn't get the results he desires, the child becomes discouraged and then turns his efforts toward another goal: gaining power. If his attempts to be powerful (to control his parents) fail, he becomes still more discouraged and his goal may become revenge.

Getting attention, power, or revenge are three basic motivations for a child's behavior. Most children concentrate on gaining attention or power; they seldom reach the revenge stage. Those who do often end up in prison or other correctional institutions.

As a child develops her own unique life-style by pursuing her basic goal, she also develops a *life theme*. The complete psychological definition of a life theme, or what some counselors call a *lifeline,* could get a bit too involved and time consuming to wade through, particularly for someone in the midst of blended family problems. For simplicity's sake, just think of a life theme as a personal motto or slogan, ideas that you repeat to yourself daily and *believe with all your heart.*

A life theme always has to do with your self-image and your sense of self-worth. I like to describe anyone's life theme in terms of "I only count when . . ." The way you finish that sentence will tell me about your life-style and will give me some definite clues about your birth order.

Controllers and Pleasers and Martyrs, Oh, My!

While everyone's life-style is different to some degree, there are broad categories into which most of the people I counsel fit: controller, pleaser, martyr, and attention-getter among others.

Controllers are powerful people who operate from one of two motivations. Their strong need for power motivates some to want to control everything and everyone. Nothing escapes their critical eye; no one they deal with is free from the strings they try to attach.

Another kind of controller, however, operates out of fear. This person is on the defensive and is basically out to be sure no one takes control of him! Controllers are more comfortable with people at arm's length. They avoid intimacy because they fear losing control. Not surprisingly, controllers tend to fear death because, after all, death is the ultimate loss of control.

Another characteristic of controllers (and remember, a controller doesn't necessarily have all the characteristics mentioned here) is a critical, perfectionistic approach. They're always trying to clear the high jump bar of life and making those around them clear it as well. Naturally, controllers have a tremendous need to be right. They love to argue, and they seldom lose an argument.

While it may sound as if controllers are aggressive, assertive people, they can also be temperamental, insecure, and shy. They may manipulate others—particularly their families—with tears or temper tantrums—or both. Whatever their weapons, they are always operating from a position of power.

Some controllers pound the table, shout, even scream. Others work quietly and may seem gentle, even loving on the surface. Underneath, however, it's a different story. A controlling mom can dominate her family by worrying about everyone. A controlling dad may keep everybody under his thumb with his silence, refusing to say what's on his mind. Fearing the unknown, the rest of the family walks on eggshells around him.

Typical life themes for controllers include the following:

- "I only count when I'm in total control of the situation."

- "I only count when I'm in charge."

- "I only count when I'm running the show, when what I say goes."

One hundred and eighty degrees from the controller is the *pleaser*. As you might guess, controllers are often married to pleasers, and we'll look at that more closely in chapter 7.

A driving force behind the pleaser is the need to be liked by everyone. Pleasers try to keep the oceans of life smooth so that they can gain everyone's approval—particularly in their families.

Pleasers typically have a poor self-image. That's why they're always trying to do everything they can to keep everyone else happy. They believe they're valued for what they do, not for who they are. They live behind masks, smiling and nodding agreement, but inside they may not agree at all; and often they're hating themselves because they don't have the courage to speak up.

Speaking up is something a pleaser seldom does because he knows that's the sure route to rejection. Pleasers much prefer to go along with others. They become skilled socially, able to read signals that others send and knowing how to keep everyone happy.

Pleasers, by the way, can be perfectionists, but they work out their perfectionism differently from controllers. They are constantly worried about measuring up, being good enough, being perfect. You might say they are perfectionists out of fear of being anything else.

Life themes for pleasers can include the following:

- "I only count when I keep everything smooth and on an even keel."

- "I only count when everyone likes me."

- "I only count when everyone approves of what I do."

- "I only count when I put others first."

Among clients from the churchgoing community I often hear the life theme "I only count when I please God and make Him happy." Instead of having a healthy desire to please God, these men and women are so perfectionistic they see God as a harsh taskmaster who demands flawless perfection from them. Serving this kind of God is a perfect way to wind up perfectly depressed.

Beyond the pleasers, you will find *martyrs*. These people almost always have a poor self-image and, naturally, they seek out others who will reinforce that poor self-image, primarily the people they marry.

Martyrs have an uncanny ability to find losers who

will walk on them, use them, or abuse them in some way. Martyrs often wind up married to alcoholics, and they tend to enable their alcoholic mates by making excuses for them out of "love."

Martyrs learn to be doormats while growing up, usually from fathers who were very strict, possessive, and controlling. Martyr wives often have husbands who wander, who have left them, or who are planning to leave them for other women. The reason is simple: a martyr isn't worth pursuing. A doormat finally gets tiresome and worn out.

While victims suffer for just about any reason, martyrs need a cause. The martyr wife makes excuses for her husband, vowing to "stand by her man" to the bitter end—and the end usually is bitter. I often deal with martyr wives from the church community who have been taught to be submissive to their husbands. At best, their interpretation of this teaching enables their controlling (and often chauvinistic) spouses to take advantage of them. At worst, they become victims of disrespect, neglect, and abuse.

The life themes I often hear from martyrs include the following:

- "I only count when I suffer."

- "I only count when I'm taken advantage of."

- "I only count when I'm hurt by others."

Close cousin to the martyr is the *victim*. The victim's life theme is very similar to the martyr's. Victims or martyrs could be called super pleasers, or pleasers who have gone to seed. Victims, martyrs, and pleasers all have the same problem—low self-esteem. In victims and martyrs, the problem is simply much worse.

The victim is sometimes called a disaster waiting to happen. Victims frequently use words like *me, my,* and *I* as they seek sympathy or pity while complaining about their misfortunes, aches, and pains. They often feel taken advantage of, but through all their complaining, they get what they really want—to be the center of attention.

The other broad life-style category I mentioned is *attention-getter,* which has some similarities to the controller. Whenever you're gaining attention you are trying to take control to some extent. Last borns of the family often have this life-style because they are the powerful little buzzards of the family who are desperately seeking lots of attention, mainly because they see all those bigger buzzards (their siblings) circling above them in a rather intimidating way.

My own life-style is primarily attention-getter because when I was very young, I perceived that I could never outdo my super capable firstborn sister or my big brother, who, although born second, was John *Junior,* the firstborn boy in the Leman family and a powerhouse in his own right. Obviously, I had to take a different route. Because it was easy and fun, I chose to become the family clown.

My life-style was pretty well set by the time I was five or six. (I'm not exactly sure because no psychologist dropped by to ask.) After that, it was all downhill, so to speak, and whatever happened only confirmed my belief that I had to be funny and cute or a mischief maker. My life theme became: "I only count when I gain attention by being entertaining." Other life themes of attention-getters include the following or variations thereof:

- "I only count when I'm in the spotlight."
- "I only count when I'm the star."
- "I only count when I make people laugh."

There are many other life-styles. A few of the more basic ones include *driver,* the goal oriented person who must reach his objective at any cost. His life theme reads, "I only count when I achieve," or "I only count when I get everything done."

Another life-style I see quite often is the *rationalizer,* an intellectual type who tries to avoid or deny his emotions by throwing up a smoke screen of theory, facts, and opinions and refuses to expose his real feelings. The rationalizer's life theme could be "I only count when I can think things through and give reasons for my behavior."

One other life-style that pops up often is the *goody-goody,* first cousin to the pleaser. The goody-goody's life theme might be "I only count when I follow the rules," or "I only count when I live a righteous life."

Later in this chapter, I will show you how to use a life-style analysis exercise to determine your own life theme as well as the life themes of others in your blended family. With only a rudimentary understanding of life-styles and life themes, you will be equipped with a useful tool to help you deal with the problems that living in a stepfamily is bound to bring. You can use this tool to avoid being stepped on or stepping on others.

Now that we have the basic information regarding

life-styles and life themes, let's see how all these elements affect the blended family. First, we will look at a "horror story" in which blended family members are having or causing serious problems. Second, we'll examine a typical "life in the trenches" blended family, in which there is tension but everyone is coping on a "two steps forward, one step backward" basis.

How Candy Tried to "Unblend" Her Family

When firstborn Ann married Ken, a mild-mannered middle child, she knew she hadn't died, but she felt she was in heaven on earth after enduring her first husband, Ron, for twelve years. After repeated physical abuse and unfaithfulness, she dissolved her marriage and received custody of their three children, Sherry, Matthew, and Eric.

When she met Ken, she knew for the first time what it was like to be with a gentle and truly caring man. Ken had joint custody of his two children, Candy and William. When Ann and Ken married, their blended family diagram looked like this:

Ann (aggressive first-born)	Ken (peaceful middle child)
Sherry—12	Candy—12
Matthew—10	William—8
Eric—6	

Ann and Ken were an unusual combination: female controller and male pleaser. Whenever I mention at seminars that some pleasers are males, I get quizzical looks from a lot of women in the audience who obviously don't believe me. I comment, "Regarding male pleasers, there are, by latest official count, nineteen pleaser husbands in the continental United States. We are not, however, releasing their names and addresses at this time." Everyone has a chuckle and my point is well made: Male pleasers are pretty rare birds.

Controlling females are a little more plentiful than male pleasers, and Ann was one of them. A firstborn who always had a lot of responsibility, Ann was six when her parents divorced. That meant Ann was frequently asked to take care of her younger brother and sister. But even before her parents' divorce, Ann had been mothering her younger sister and baby brother, firmly entrenched in the firstborn role of being responsible. It's no wonder, then, that she developed a controller lifestyle and a life theme that said, "I only count when I take charge."

Her new husband, Ken, was a typical middle child, with a brother three years older who had had no trouble maintaining his firstborn position; he was the star athlete of the family and a fairly good student to boot. Ken, on the other hand, went in other directions, finding fulfillment in being the family entrepreneur and starting several "small businesses" even as a child.

Ken often found himself mediating between his older brother, Harold, and little brother, Ralph. Little Ralphie seemed to take particular delight in setting up Harold, who tended to be short of patience with little twerps who "got in his stuff." Ken always tried to help them work things out, and when necessary, he would hide Ralphie until Harold cooled off. Ken's life theme was predictable enough: "I only count when I get along with others and make things smooth for everyone."

Custody on Alternating Weeks = A Nightmare

After a twelve-year marriage, Ken's first wife decided he couldn't provide all the things she needed, so she filed for divorce. Every now and then, for reasons known only to them, judges decide the best custody situation is to give the children to the parents on an "equal basis." In the case of Ken and his ex-wife, they had the children on alternating weeks, a totally unworkable situation at best that predictably enough turned into a nightmare.

In fact, the word *nightmare* pretty well sums up the first year that Ken and his new family tried to blend. The twelve-year-old stepsisters had to share a room, and because Ann's daughter, Sherry, was a neatnik and Ken's daughter, Candy, was a slob, they had many disagreements and even fights. Sherry, a compliant pleaser, was no match for tough-talking Candy, and she usually lost.

Like her mother, Sherry had grown up as the firstborn responsible one and had wound up often caring for Eric, her baby brother. Although a firstborn, Sherry had become discouraged by her aggressive mom to whom she could never measure up. She had developed a compliant personality, and her pleaser life theme read, "I only count when people like me."

Candy, on the other hand, grew up parented by Ken, the peaceful middle child who, unfortunately, was more than a little permissive. The squabbles between the girls usually wound up with Candy calling Sherry four-letter names; then both girls would sulk for hours after Ken and Ann tried to calm them down.

There were several reasons for Candy's bad temper. For one thing, she was a discouraged perfectionist who had never been able to emulate her natural mother,

Mimi, a firstborn and a fanatic about keeping her house clean. Nor was Candy able to follow in the footsteps of her easygoing, smooth talking dad, who always seemed to have things together. Instead, she picked up her mother's critical eye and developed a sharp tongue and a disdain for authority. A classic rebel with no particular cause, Candy's life theme said, "I only count when I get my way."

Matt, Ann's middle child and the firstborn son in the family, had carved out his own niche as a good student with a friendly, outgoing nature that won him many friends. While he didn't have a grade point average as high as his sister's, he did quite well. *Balanced* was a good word for Matt, and his life theme was "I only count when I please my friends."

Matt shared a room with his little brother, Eric, who had the classic life theme of many a last born: "I only count when I entertain." The Chevy Chase of the family, Eric usually had everyone in stitches—that is, everyone but his stepsiblings, Candy and William.

Candy ignored Eric, referring to him as "the chubby little twerp," but William, who had been the baby of the family before the blending was a different matter. He thought Eric was not funny at all and was always on his case for alleged invasions of his room and his things.

Although a last born, four years younger than his very aggressive sister, William was also the firstborn male in his original family. He had learned to hold his own with Candy even though she was always writing him off as "too little and too dumb." A big clue to William's personality is that his family called him William, not Billy. His life theme was clear: "I only count when I stand up for my rights."

Ann and Candy Bumped Heads
the Most

With all those life themes crisscrossing each other in more ways than one, the first year was chaos. It didn't help at all when Candy and William would leave every other Friday and not return until the following Thursday night to stay for another week. Typically, it took two or three days for Candy and William to settle back into the family routine. At their mom's house, they had little or no discipline and could watch anything they wanted on TV, staying up as long as they liked.

Ann, who was used to running a tight ship, constantly bumped heads with both of her stepchildren, particularly Candy. Her naive fantasy about being a good stepmother was shattered when Candy started screaming four-letter words in her face on a regular basis.

Candy never accepted her father's remarriage and plotted to break it up in any way she could. Just before she turned sixteen, she thought she found a way. She began dating an eighteen-year-old senior in her high school and was soon sexually active with him. One day Ann caught them having sex in her bed. Distressed and shocked, she called Ken to let him know what his daughter had been up to. Ken came home from work immediately. He spent time calming Ann down before they talked with Candy, who was sullen and defiant.

Candy Had Her Own Way to
"Spit in the Soup"

Ann could tell that Candy was actually pleased that she'd been caught having sex in the bed where her stepmother slept with her father. It was her way of "spitting in the soup" and gaining a small measure of revenge.

With her controller's mentality, Candy had decided, "If my dad has the right to hurt me by getting divorced, I have the right to hurt him back." So she struck back at her dad by being promiscuous. She also admitted thinking that if she caused enough trouble, Dad would see the error of his ways and come back home.

When Ken's ex-wife, Mimi, heard about Candy's sexual escapades with the eighteen-year-old senior, she wanted the boy prosecuted for statutory rape. Ken managed to talk his ex-wife out of that idea, arguing that it could do more harm than good. Squelching her desire to "belt Candy one," Ann joined Ken in trying to help Candy as well as the young man. They even arranged some counseling for him since his own parents, both alcoholics, couldn't have cared less about what he was doing.

Much to Candy's chagrin, her sexual adventures didn't shake the marriage of her dad and her stepmother at all; if anything, their relationship seemed to become stronger. A year later, Candy found a new boyfriend and tried the same thing again, with the same result. What Candy didn't count on was the fact that Ann and Ken were solid allies, totally committed to their marriage no matter what happened with their children.

At the time I interviewed Ann, she and Ken had been married for four years. Ken's ex-wife had moved out of state, and Candy had chosen to move in with her mom on a full-time basis. Ann and Ken had agreed to let her do so for a year to see how it went, but they were apprehensive.

One bright spot for the family was that Ann had gained Candy's respect by being loving but firm. The supposedly wicked stepmother had earned her stripes to the extent that Candy decided to take some advice Ann gave her just before she moved in with her mother: that she pick her friends more wisely. Candy had been hanging around with a couple of girls who had been very bad influences.

Surprisingly, after Candy moved in with her mother, she had been befriended by a couple of very responsible girls in her new high school. They had urged her to join them in trying out for the girls' basketball team, and Candy had worked her way up to starting forward. Ann and Ken were pleased with Candy's new maturity, but they still had their doubts.

Ann and Ken have faced plenty of nightmares and have their horror stories to tell; their marriage has come through intact only because they were absolutely committed to one another at the start. In fact, Candy should have known better than to try to undermine their relationship. At the very beginning, Ken and Ann had told all five of the children on several occasions in different ways: "Don't try to drive a wedge between us because, even though we love you, we are committed to being married." Their strong marriage had helped their blended family weather the storm. In chapter 7, we'll come back to Ken and Ann to learn about a valuable tool they used to keep their marriage strong.

"Our Four Sons" and New Baby Makes Five

Not every family faces nightmares like those Ken and Ann endured. For Charles and Teresa, it was a matter of just surviving day-to-day living. Teresa was a middle child from a religious family. She had grown up thinking, "I only count when I please God—and my dad." A classic pleaser, Teresa tried all her life to keep everyone happy by balancing and smoothing things whenever she could. But even a Diehard battery runs down eventually, and she was just about out of energy. In a word, Teresa was tired.

Her second husband, Charles, was an only child, retired from the military, and while he was a loving good-hearted man, he still operated as if he were giving orders to a platoon. He was an only child because his parents had planned it that way, so from the very start he was used to a tightly structured, highly disciplined environment. He had taken quite well to military service, and he still liked to bellow orders like a buck sergeant. Charles's life theme plainly added up to, "I only count when I'm in charge and running things *right!*"

Teresa's first marriage failed because she fell into the hands of a ruthless controller who was committed only to what he wanted to do. Eventually he decided he didn't want to continue to be a husband and father. He walked out on Teresa and her two sons when Rex was two and Scott was only a few months old. Today he lives at the other end of the country and contacts his ex-wife and kids on only rare occasions, sending only Christmas cards and occasional brief notes.

Charles also brought two boys to the marriage, James and Jon. Little Emily, a daughter born to Teresa and Charles the first year they were married, completed a family diagram that looked like this:

Teresa (middle child pleaser)	Charles (only child controller, bark worse than bite)
Rex—7	James—8
Scott—5	Jon—6
Emily—19 months	

In this blended family, everybody was on a collision course. Rex, Teresa's older son, was the family jock, gifted in just about any sport he wanted to try. At seven, he had already settled on his life theme: "I only count when I win."

On the other side was Rex's stepcounterpart, James, who had snapped to for his overbearing dad ever since he could remember. He knew his father loved him, but he was still afraid of him. A true firstborn, James's life theme proclaimed, "I only count when I toe the line." With his dad for a role model, young James had become a controller in his own right, and he was constantly trying to control the other children in the family.

Did the two firstborns in this blended family fight? Do cub bears climb trees? Although James was a year older, two inches taller, and twenty pounds heavier, Rex could run circles around him whenever they competed at anything. And when James got fed up and tried to assert his authority as the oldest with a shove or even a punch, Rex cleaned his clock.

As for Jon, Charles's younger son, he hadn't been as obedient as his older brother. Built a lot like his step-brother Rex, but not as coordinated, Jon was more wary than Rex of his big brother's superior size and strength. Jon was biding his time, living in the shadow of his older brother but wanting to make his mark. And when his father married Teresa and Rex and Scott appeared, his resentment just increased. Jon's life-style was a mix that is not all that unusual—attention-getter/martyr—and his life theme said, "I only count when I show others I'm important."

And, of course, the person that Jon resented the most was Scott, who at age four took over as the blended family baby—for nine months, anyway. Then Emily arrived (conceived on the honeymoon), and Scott not only had to keep his eyes open to avoid Jon's wrath, but he suffered the pains of being dethroned by little Baby Princess.

Scott did not appreciate his position in his new blended family at all. He was a powerful little buzzard who had gloried in his role as the baby of his natural family before the divorce. His life theme was "I only count when I'm the center of attention." Then along came Jon, who started giving him problems. The last straw was little Emily, who took the spotlight totally off of him.

Scott, the Clingy Controller

Instead of throwing temper tantrums, Scott used different weapons to compete and be powerful. During the first few months of Emily's life, Scott became very whiny and possessive of his mother, clinging to her leg and even begging her to feed him. Scott was working hard developing his own brand of the controller/attention-getter life-style and giving Emily a bad time whenever he could get away with it.

Scott was a little bit like the wide receiver who goes out for a pass and, just as he's about to catch the ball, hears footsteps behind him. Scott was always looking over his shoulder, seeing his little sister coming up from behind, blossoming before his very eyes, getting the attention of his parents and his grandparents.

Scott had said to himself in so many words, "Hey, wait a minute, I'm no slouch at getting attention myself, and with all this competition I'll take it a step further. I'll make *sure* they pay attention to me."

The clinging and whiny behavior that Scott chose may

seem weak, but it is a sign of a powerful controller. I can always spot a controlling kid. His mother limps into my office dragging one leg because her child is firmly attached to it, clinging with all his might. In Scott's case, he doesn't want to share the big pie of attention with his new little sister. His strategy was clearly, "How can Mom not notice me? I've got her by the leg."

Pluses Among the Minuses

For Teresa and Charles, it had been two steps forward and one step back with their blended family. They had some pluses going for them. As a middle child and a people person, Teresa really did have a fairly good relationship with her stepsons. In fact, the boys often went to her for encouragement and support because they were reluctant to approach their father. Even though James fought with Teresa's son Rex, Teresa was able to keep everyone's good will because she was fair and loving all around.

Another plus was the arrival of little Emily, who had been greeted with approval by all the boys except for Scott, the displaced baby of the family. What Charles and Teresa needed to work on was helping Scott get over the hump of feeling displaced.

The child in this family who was paying the highest price was James. His "toe the line" life theme put a lot of pressure on him, and when he tried to pressure others, he was rebuffed, particularly by Rex, who though younger and smaller was a lot tougher. From her vantage point as stepmother, Teresa needed to do all she could to help Charles lighten up on James and Jon, and at the same time she had to be careful not to move in too fast on her stepsons, particularly in areas of discipline. (We'll discuss discipline more in chapter 9.)

Everyone in the Blender
Sees Life Differently

As you assess your own blended family, you can learn a lot about how to deal with everyone by determining, from your perspective at least, the life theme for each member, including your spouse.

Granted, it is impossible to read the mind of another person and precisely state that person's life-style or life theme. But what is helpful in this kind of exercise is that you put down what you *perceive* is the life theme of your spouse, your children, and your stepchildren. As you postulate a life theme for everyone in your family, it will give you a much better idea how to understand and relate to each person.

To see how a life theme analysis would work, let's go back and look at the blended family of Teresa and Charles who each brought two sons to the new marriage. Later they had a daughter, Emily, now only nineteen months old.

Teresa (pleaser): "I only count when I please God—and my dad."

Charles (controller): "I only count when I'm in charge and running things *right!*"

Rex, 7 (driver/controller): "I only count when I win."

James, 8 (goody-goody/controller): "I only count when I toe the line."

Scott, 5 (controller/attention-getter): "I only count when I'm the center of attention."

Jon, 6 (attention-getter/martyr): "I only count when I show others I'm important."

Emily, 19 months: Life-style development in progress; seems to be doing daily auditions for the star role of baby princess of the family.

Using the above diagram for an example, try describing your own family in terms of life-style and life theme. Start with yourself and go on to describe how you experience other family members.

1. *What words below would best describe your life-style? If you feel that you have characteristics that fit more than one description, check them both off but put a big "X" by the one that is predominant. Then write down your life-style, putting the predominant description first.*

_____ *Controller*
_____ *Perfectionist*
_____ *Driver*
_____ *Pleaser*
_____ *Victim*
_____ *Martyr*
_____ *Goody-goody*
_____ *Attention-getter*
_____ *Rationalizer*

2. *My life theme is as follows:*
"*I only count when* _____."

3. *Using the life-styles listed in exercise 1, give your own estimate of which ones apply to your spouse (remember, you can use more than one style, but write the predominant one first):* _____.

4. *From the descriptions that you have given of your spouse above, state what you believe is your spouse's life theme:*
"I only count when _____."

5. *Next, describe your own children in terms of life-styles and life themes:*
"My firstborn's life-style is _____."
His or her life theme seems to be "I only count when _____

_____."
"My second born's life-style is _____."
His or her life theme seems to be "I only count when _____

_____."
My last born's life-style is _____."
His or her life theme seems to be "I only count when _____

_____."
(If you have more than three children, pencil in the appropriate information.)

6. *Next, describe your stepchildren in terms of life-style and life theme:*
"My firstborn stepchild's life-style is _____."
His or her life theme seems to be "I only count when _____

_____."
"My second born stepchild's life-style is _____."
His or her life theme seems to be "I only count

when _____
_____."

"*My last born stepchild's life-style is* _____."
His or her life theme seems to be "I only count
when _____
_____."

(If you have more than three stepchildren, pencil in
the appropriate information.)

Now look back over your answers. If you find words
like *very, really,* and *extremely,* you may be a perfectionist and a fault finder. If you didn't check off the perfectionist life-style for yourself, you may want to go back
and reassess your personality. Remember, we all tend to
lie to ourselves, but only the truth is really going to help.

Share Perceptions with Family Members

If any of your children are mature teenagers, you
might want to share your perceptions with them and get
their feedback. You might also want them to write down
their perceptions of you. But do this only if you are
confident that it will enhance your relationship to each
child and not cause tension or hard feelings.

The best person with whom to share this life-style
analysis exercise is your spouse. Use it as a means of
building better communication between the two of you,
which is essential for facing the challenge of blending a
family. For most couples, this challenge can seem insurmountable at times. Remarried couples must do everything they can to understand who they are as well as
who their children and stepchildren are in order to help
their blended family not only survive but also succeed.

The foundation of every blended family is the marriage of the man and woman who decide they are willing to try marriage again. It's so important, I'll put it bluntly:

*Without a strong marriage,
your blended family is
in big-time trouble.*

In Part 2, we will see why this warning is true and discuss what you and your spouse can do to keep your marriage healthy.

NOTES

1. Alfred Adler, *The Practice and Theory of Individual Psychology* (London: Routledge & Kegan Paul, Ltd., 1923), 3.

2. Alfred Adler, *Understanding Human Nature* (Greenwich, CT: Fawcett Publications, Inc., 1927), 31.

3. See Rudolph Dreikurs, *Fundamentals of Adlerian Psychology* (Chicago: Alfred Adler Institute, 1953), 35.

PART TWO

You and Your Spouse Must BLEND FIRST

CHAPTER 7

Husbands and Wives

The Most Important Birth Order Blend of All

As I talk with spouses from blended families, I often ask them if the pop song Frank Sinatra made famous in the early '60s is true: "Is love lovelier the second time around?" I get a lot of quizzical looks, a few wry smiles, and very few *absolutely!*'s. Instead, I'm told, *The second time around love must be wiser—and stronger.*

Some wives were just plain blunt about the difficulties they discovered in remarrying and blending families. Typical was Rita, who, when asked what she had learned from her second marriage into a stepfamily, said: "My first response is don't remarry. Remarriage is very, very difficult . . . it's just tough from the beginning, it's the hardest way to go."

When Rita married Wally, she thought they had made a lot of right moves. "I had been single for five years after my first husband left me," Rita explained. "I really tried to plan it all carefully. I met Wally at a Parents

Without Partners meeting, and when we seemed to hit it off, we decided to go into marriage absolutely committed to one another. We had both been through divorce, and we didn't want it to happen again. We went to premarital counseling at his church, which was compatible with my own beliefs. But despite all that planning, I have to say it didn't prepare me for what happened."

Wally had come to the marriage with no children, and when I observed that they should have had an easier time blending, Rita just laughed and said, "That's the way it looked to us before we got married, but it isn't the way it turned out. Blending Wally with my kids has been really difficult, and I'm not convinced that he and I are blending very well, either."

The story Rita told was typical of so many I've heard before. The Prince who seemed to be so agreeable, loving, and attentive before marriage turned into a frog afterward. Wally's "real personality" came to the surface, and he turned out to be a controller who believed in a very authoritarian approach to raising children.

Rita's children did not adjust well to this new father figure who suddenly arrived in their home playing the role of a strict disciplinarian without first establishing any relationships. When they rejected him, Wally couldn't understand why. He had agreed to some family counseling sessions, but they had done little good because he refused to budge from his position that he didn't have to win over the children. He felt they should submit to him simply because he was "the head of the house."

"Obviously, Wally doesn't understand what it means to be a stepparent," I commented. "He doesn't think it's necessary to earn the right to be heard."

"You know, Wally had all the right answers when we went for premarital counseling," Rita said with a frustrated laugh. "And he was polite—even nice—to my kids when we were dating, but then we got married. Until you live with someone every day, you and your children all together under the same roof, you don't know what you're going to cope with. Wally thinks my kids must obey his every command simply because he's my husband and their stepfather."

"Is Wally a good husband in other areas?" I asked.

"Another big problem we have is that Wally tries to control all the money. When we got married, he made me quit my job. Now, he doles out a little money at a time, and I have to account for every penny."

"And what has been your response to that?"

"Up until now I've been the good wife who tries to make everybody happy. I talk about marriage being oneness—loving and nurturing each other as we are one. He seems to think that oneness is going to work, coming home, providing food, and paying the bills. Well, that's not oneness as far as I'm concerned."

"Wally isn't unusual," I said. "A lot of men equate provision with love. Before we go any further, I'd like to know your birth order as well as Wally's. I've got a hunch I already know, but tell me anyway."

"I'm a firstborn—I have a brother two years younger," Rita said. "Wally is also a firstborn—he has two younger brothers."

"Bingo!" I responded. "You and Wally have a birth order combination that can cause problems—two first-borns who are bumping heads in a lot of ways."

"Are you saying our problems are due to our birth orders?" Rita asked incredulously.

"It's not the whole answer, but the fact that you're both firstborns has pointed you in that direction. There are many firstborn couples who have a good marriage, but when a firstborn marries another firstborn, there are certain things they must look out for and work on."

As I diagrammed Rita's family, her problem became more clear to her.

Rita (firstborn pleaser)	Wally (firstborn con-
Amy—12	troller)
Amanda—10	No children
Alex—8	

I often liken marriage to two people trying to play the same game with different rule books. Each spouse walks into the marriage with his or her own rule book, which is based on the life-style and life theme each one has developed after being born into a special spot in his or her family. Few engaged couples ever exchange rule books or talk about them, even if they go to premarital counseling. Once they say, "I do," each spouse begins operating within the marriage according to a very personal set of rules.

It doesn't take long, however, to discover that your spouse's rule book sounds like something from a foreign land. It's not a matter of deciding whose rule book is right and whose rule book is wrong. The real challenge is for each spouse to translate his or her rule book to the other in such a way that they can achieve harmony and understanding.

This is easily said, not easily done. By the time someone marries, his or her life-style has been established for years. The grain of the wood is set, and there is no changing it. You can reshape the wood, sometimes substantially by modifying your behavior and learning how to correct your weaknesses while capitalizing on your strengths; but you cannot change the grain. Your basic life-style is there for life.

That Rita and Wally were having problems was no surprise. Having never had children, Wally, the consummate controller, was bound to think his word would be law when he moved in with Rita and her kids. But what Wally hadn't understood is that he had married another *firstborn*, and while she seemed compliant enough, she still had some characteristics that finally caused her to resist his controlling ways.

Although Rita's life theme read, "I only count when I make everybody happy," she had been doing a slow boil for so long that it was getting to her. A compliant pleaser, she still had firstborn traits of stubbornness and her own brand of perfectionism. She was also prone to moodiness, and she was running out of energy fighting battles with Wally, who couldn't understand how he could have married into such an uncooperative buzz saw. Why couldn't Rita and her kids realize that he was out there breaking his neck to provide for all of them?

Controllers and Pleasers Often Marry

Wally and Rita epitomized the two life-styles I counsel most: controllers and pleasers. Controllers are, more often than not, men who give their pleaser wives a bad time. It's hard to get a controlling husband to my office for counseling because he's sure that his wife is the one with the problem; there's nothing wrong with *him*.

But when the controller finally agrees to come in and talk to me, he lets his true colors show in a hurry. I hear statements that add up to life themes like these:

"I only count when . . . I'm in charge . . . when what I say goes . . . when I'm running things."

To help my clients recognize if they are dating a controller or if they are, indeed, married to one, I've developed the following quiz. If you suspect you might be married to a controller, go through the following questions, but don't mark them simply yes or no. Score a 4 for *always;* 3 for *often;* 2 for *sometimes;* and 1 for *seldom.*

The Telltale Signs of a Controller

_____ 1. He tends to be critical—a fault-finding perfectionist with a high standard of excellence for himself and others.

_____ 2. He finds it difficult to laugh at himself, particularly when he may have done or said something awkward or wrong.

_____ 3. He puts down or degrades others with subtle or not-so-subtle humor.

_____ 4. He has a weak (or even a poor) relationship with his mother (or other women who have been, or still are, part of his life, such as a sister or a supervisor).

_____ 5. He complains about authority figures who "don't know what they are doing" (employers, teachers, pastors, or the president).

_____ 6. He is a "real competitor" who always has to win at sports or table games.

_____ 7. He gets his way, subtly or not so subtly, about where the two of you will go or what you will do.

_____ 8. He prefers to run the show rather than be a team player—on the job, in committees, or in situations involving family or friends.

_____ 9. *He has a hard time saying "I was wrong" or makes excuses that will make him look good in the face of adversity.*

_____10. *He loses his temper (raises his voice, screams, curses).*

_____11. *He can get physical—shoving or hitting you or smashing things.*

_____12. *He makes you account for every penny you spend but spends rather freely himself.*

_____13. *Sex is something the two of you engage in for his pleasure and at his convenience.*

_____14. *When he drinks alcohol, even in modest quantities, he starts to become a different person.*

_____15. *He makes excuses for excessive drinking.*

No pop quiz like this can be absolute proof of anything, but it can give you some clues that might help you analyze your relationship to your spouse. If the ratings you gave your spouse add up to between 50 and 60, he is a super controller—whose only hope is a professional counselor (if he'll listen).

If you scored your husband somewhere between 40 and 49, he is a typical controller, who is probably open to being confronted and asked to change his behavior.

If you scored your husband between 30 and 39, congratulations! He should be a fairly balanced person who can be in control at times but flexible at others.

If you scored your husband at 29 or less, first recheck your figures. If you haven't made a scoring error, you may have one of the few pleaser husbands in captivity. But take a second look if he scored higher than a 2 on any of the following questions: 10, 11, 12, 13, 14. All of these suggest a high degree of need to control, even dominate, with violence and abuse.

The prey of the controller is the pleaser spouse. And because most pleasers are wives, the following questions use the feminine pronoun. Again, the scoring is the same: a 4 for *always;* a 3 for *often;* a 2 for *sometimes;* and a 1 for *seldom.*

The Telltale Signs of a Pleaser

_____ 1. *She walks on eggshells to keep everyone happy.*

_____ 2. *She wonders why she can't do things right.*

_____ 3. *She feels insecure, lacking confidence.*

_____ 4. *Her father was or is authoritarian.*

_____ 5. *She avoids confronting others because it "just isn't worth it."*

_____ 6. *She's often heard saying, "I should have . . ." or "I ought to . . ."*

_____ 7. *She feels overpowered by her spouse and even her children.*

_____ 8. *She gets little affection from others.*

_____ 9. *She feels like hiding or running away from "the hassle."*

_____10. *Her spouse and children know which buttons to press to make her feel guilty.*

_____11. *She feigns agreement or approval when she feels just the opposite on the inside.*

_____12. *She is easily persuaded by others and will go along with whomever talked to her last.*

_____13. *She is afraid to try new things or take new risks.*

_____14. *It embarrasses her to stand up for her rights or take the initiative.*

_____15. *She gets little respect from her spouse or her children.*

The spouse scoring between 50 and 60 would be considered a super suffering pleaser who could easily be in the hands of a misogynist (a woman hater who needs a professional counselor).

Anyone scoring 40 to 49 is a discouraged or depressed pleaser for whom there is hope *if* she is willing to take action and confront her husband.

Anyone scoring 30 to 39 is a mildly discouraged pleaser. Her positives in life outweigh her negatives, but she still would like a little more respect, particularly from her family.

Those scoring 29 or below fall into the "positive pleaser" category. They are able to balance their very giving nature with being able to receive the love, support, and respect they want and need.

Some Couples Weren't Born for Each Other

Studies have shown that certain birth orders do better than others in a marriage relationship.[1] If two firstborns like Wally and Rita aren't the best risk for marriage—particularly a remarriage in a blended family—what are the best combinations?

My own experience with hundreds of couples suggests that a good general rule for a happy marriage is to find someone as opposite your birth order as possible. In general, opposites not only attract—in marriage, they are good for one another.

Only children and last borns supposedly make the best match, followed by firstborns and last borns. Then come the middle children and last borns. In case you think I'm favoring last borns as the best possibilities for marriage because I'm a last born married to a firstborn, let me assure you that these findings come from research in which I took no part whatsoever. (And besides, when I once questioned these statistics myself in my wife's presence, she quickly assured me that I was indeed very happily married—so it must be true!)

While there are no guarantees that being a certain birth order means that you and your spouse will live happily—or miserably—ever after, there are indicators that show which combinations work best. Following is a quick rundown of six birth order combinations and why they tend to go wrong or right in a marriage. For more detailed information, read my book *The Birth Order Connection*.[2]

Firstborn + Firstborn = A Power Struggle

The marriage of two firstborn personalities might actually be a match between an only child and a firstborn, two only children, or two firstborns. (Since only children are super firstborns, we're including them in this group.) The issues in this kind of match usually focus on perfectionism and control.

As we have seen, perfectionists are the ones who can

spot flaws at forty yards or beyond. Put two firstborns together, both of whom are very likely to be perfectionistic, and there is bound to be a power struggle—possibly a war. In addition, two firstborn personalities can wind up butting heads because by nature they are both used to calling the shots and leading the way.

As we have seen with Rita and Wally, however, it is possible for one firstborn to be a compliant pleaser while the other one is the controller. They may not butt heads, but as the controller takes advantage of the pleaser and grinds her down, there is a power struggle of a different kind. Finally, when the pleaser's patience and energy are exhausted, divorce becomes likely.

That was the problem facing Rita and Wally when Rita contacted me. Although he had walked out on one marriage counselor, Wally agreed to see me. I was able to lead him in slow baby steps of progress, showing him that he could not come down on Rita's kids with all kinds of rules and demand their obedience when he hadn't earned the right to be heard by them. As for his relationship with his wife, Wally had to learn the key principle for any controller married to a pleaser:

Control is not love.

"If you love Rita, you won't try to control her," I told Wally. "You'll let her have more say about money and not just dole it out penny by penny to her. You'll let her be free to be the person she really is."

I also made it a point to speak to Rita alone. "If you want your marriage to really change," I told her, "you have to refuse to play Wally's controlling games. He'll always think and act like a controller, and you won't be able to change that. But you *can* deal with him. When he starts in with his controller antics, just tell him nicely, 'I'm not your secretary, I'm your wife.'"

With a little more coaching, Rita got the message, and she soon had an opportunity to cut Wally, the controller, off at the pass. In spite of what I had said to him, he continued with his "you've got to account for every dollar you spend" policy. When he started quizzing Rita about why food was so expensive and why couldn't she make the food budget stretch farther, she told him, "Honey, *you* do the shopping."

"What do you mean, *me* do the shopping?" Wally demanded with a puzzled look.

"Just what I said. I don't tell you how to service your car, and I don't expect to have you tell me how to shop for the family. You shop for this next week and learn what things cost. See for yourself what it's like."

Wally was so stunned that he could do nothing but back off for the moment. A little later, he became determined to show Rita how to shop the right way and went at his new challenge with gusto. But after one trip to the supermarket, he came home throwing his hands in the air, admitting he had no idea that groceries were priced so ridiculously high.

It took a while, but as Rita stood her ground rather than just giving in (in her usual pleaser fashion), Wally started to come around. And he learned that Rita wanted a lot more from their marriage than just to be provided for. As he began meeting Rita's need for togetherness (on my insistence, they got away for some weekends alone), he found that his sex life improved immeasurably.

The last time I saw them, I felt fairly certain that Wally and Rita would make it because they had taken their first and toughest steps toward learning how to deal with the issue of control. The pleaser was starting to assert herself, the controller was backing off, and both were happier for it.

Other Tips for Firstborn Couples

If you are a firstborn or an only child married to another firstborn or only child, here are some tips for reducing tension and increasing harmony:

1. *Steer away from "improving" on things your spouse does or says.* Because you are probably a perfectionist, doing so may be difficult, but bite your tongue and do it anyway. Practice tongue control whenever possible. The New Testament compares the tongue to the bit in a horse's mouth or the rudder in a huge ship.[3] Either device turns and controls everything. The tongue can literally turn your marriage in one direction or another.

2. *Stop "shoulding" your mate.* As a perfectionist, you are prone to be a fault-finder. Criticism is second nature to you, and not only do you criticize others, but your main target is yourself. Put away your high jump bar. Quit trying to jump higher, and quit asking your mate to do so as well.

3. *To avoid control issues, have good role definitions*—a specific division of labor as to who does what in the family. You may do the shopping but your spouse may be the one who pays the bills and balances the checking account. Try to help each other with your assigned tasks rather than compete with each other or make things difficult. For example, if one spouse controls the social calendar, the other shouldn't make commitments without checking with him or her first.

4. *Realize there are more ways to skin a cat than your way.* This tip was especially helpful to Phil and Peggy, whom you met in earlier chapters. Phil, a meticulous firstborn controller, looked on his family as if it were a business. Peggy, his only-child spouse, had grown up with few, if any, challenges of her opinion or of what she did and how she did it. Each of them needed to value the other's ideas and to learn that a suggestion that wasn't his or her own could still be a good one—even the best one—for all concerned.

Beyond that, Phil and Peggy were able to build on the many strengths they brought together as two firstborns. Because they were both logical, organized, and conscientious, they could work out their problems together. They never had to worry about the left hand not knowing what the right hand was doing.

Firstborn + Middle Born = A Need for "Tell Me More"

If you're a firstborn married to a middle born, rejoice in realizing you've married the most monogamous of all birth orders who have the best track record in building a lasting marriage. At the same time, be aware that middle children can also be a vexing paradox.

For example, while they have grown up having to learn how to negotiate, mediate, and compromise, they are also often secretive, preferring to keep their emotions close to the vest.

From the other side, if you're a middle child married to a firstborn your tendency is to just throw your spouse a bone once in a while without letting him know how you really feel. If you have difficulty articulating your feelings, try writing them down and sharing them in notes that you can discuss later with your spouse.

Also, take time to discuss your day or your week. Resist your natural tendency to keep feelings inside and open up to your firstborn spouse as you trust him or her to listen. The reason Ken and Ann were able to weather all the trouble caused by Ken's promiscuous daughter, Candy, was their "daily recaps" when they sat down and took time to check out each other's lives. Ann, the assertive firstborn controller, had to be sure she was getting everything out of Ken, whose typical response was usually, "Oh, everything's okay, I guess."

"What do you mean okay?" Ann would press gently. "Ken, I really want to know how you feel and what you think." With that kind of encouragement, Ken was able to open up about his daughter, Candy; about problems at work; and about whatever else was on his mind.

Daily recaps—or at least a recap every few days—are valuable to any marriage, but they are particularly useful when one mate tends to be less inclined to share feelings. Ken and Ann sometimes did their recapping while taking a walk to talk about the sermon they had heard that Sunday at church. Discussing their spiritual beliefs and the values they wanted to hold onto was a major source of strength during their blended family storms.

Teresa Had Settled for Peace at Any Price

Besides being "bone tossers," middle borns are often pleasers who are willing to settle for peace at any price. Teresa, the middle-child wife of Charles, the loving controller who bellowed like a buck sergeant, was a good example. Teresa, you may recall, shied away from head-on confrontations with Charles, but she was an excellent negotiator and mediator with her children. She was particularly skilled at listening to Charles's sons, James and Jon, who were afraid to "bother Dad."

At the same time, Teresa hesitated to tell Charles how she felt about all the family tensions—the fights between Charles's son James and her boy Rex and the antics of Scott, her displaced five-year-old, who was now clinging to her and whining for attention because of little Emily, the nineteen-month-old bundle of joy born nine months after Teresa and Charles's marriage.

When I gave Charles the Telltale Signs of a Controller quiz, he scored 41, which indicated that there was hope for him to make some changes rather quickly if he wanted to. Fortunately, he did want to because although he was controlling, he was a benevolent dictator who used a loud voice only out of habit from his years in the military.

Through counseling, Charles learned to become quite good at consulting Teresa and the children before making decisions that directly, or even indirectly, affected them. On top of that, he made a vow to pace himself and deal with things as they came up rather than let them accumulate to the point at which they would cause him to blow up.

But what about Charles's loud tone, which he used on many occasions without even realizing it? With Teresa's help, he was soon able to reflect on how he felt as a kid when his own parents shouted at him. He made a pact with his family to talk more softly and gave permission to everyone to let him know when he started to get too loud. His younger boy, Jon, came up with the perfect signal. "Dad, when you get too loud, we're just going to put our hands over our ears!"

Other Tips for Firstborns and Middles

Here are some practical suggestions for firstborns married to middles.

1. *Treat your middle child spouse special.* Give small gifts, write love notes, say the things he or she needs to hear. (More on this in chapter 8.) Any time you do things to make a middle child feel special you are scoring points because it's a fairly good bet he wasn't made to feel all that special while growing up.

2. *Work at getting your middle child spouse to articulate feelings.* By nature, firstborns are impatient know-it-alls, so back off of that tendency and keep asking your middle child spouse, "What do you think?" "Tell me how you really feel," or "Tell me more." The husband of a middle-child wife often has two good reasons to seek out her opinion: First, she is probably more perceptive than he is regarding people and their feelings. Second, she's comfortable in the middle, where she can be solving and mediating problems, smoothing the way for everyone.

3. *Always assure middle child spouses that their qualities and skills are useful and needed.* In a blended family, this can mean encouraging the middle child to use negotiating skills, especially on those Armageddon-like evenings when stepsiblings are battling it out. Because she's a middle child, she is probably best equipped to see both sides of a conflict and call the shots correctly.

Firstborn + Last Born = Bliss (Usually)

According to one study of three thousand families done by birth order specialist Walter Toman, the odds are best for a happy marriage when a firstborn hooks up with a last born.[4] The theory at work here is that the firstborn can teach the last born little things that are probably lacking in his or her life, like being organized, having goals and plans, and that he or she has to get serious now and then.

Strangely enough, the rather huge differences between the firstborn and the last born seem to balance each other much like two people of equal weight on a teeter-totter. And it helps if the firstborn can choose a last born who, while being full of life and fun, is a little more "together." One of the best examples I've seen recently of a beautiful firstborn/last born blend is Connie Sellecca, star of various TV series, including *Hotel* and more recently *Second Chances,* and John Tesh, star of *Entertainment Tonight.*

With two older sisters, John is the baby of his family, and Connie has so many firstborn traits I'd bet my birth order decoder ring that she is at least a firstborn girl—perhaps even an only child.

In an article featured on the cover of a national women's magazine, Connie and John shared some lessons in love which have helped their marriage succeed when a lot of Hollywood observers thought it was doomed for failure because both had had such unhappy first marriages, both had volatile temperaments, and both were work and career oriented. There was also the matter of Connie's son, Gib, who was twelve when they were considering marriage and who had had his mom to himself for quite a few years while she had been a single parent.

But after a year and a half, with a baby on the way, their marriage was working beautifully for several reasons. Connie, who possessed typical firstborn strengths, such as being very organized and meticulous, made it a point to control her work schedule so that it didn't encroach on family life. She also taught John, a hang-loose last born, how important the family is. He says, "I learned that Connie and Gib are my family, and my family always comes first. Really good things come from the love I get from them."[5]

While Connie has done her best to organize John and help him get his priorities straight, his laid-back, mellow approach to life has helped her relax and enjoy their life together. The only boy in his family, John was an excellent candidate for marriage because his big sisters had taught him firsthand about what women are like and what makes them tick. Early in their marriage, John perceived what would irritate Connie and worked hard at not intentionally doing those little things that would drive her crazy. Connie has said to her mother-in-law, "I owe you so big; you gave me the perfect husband. I'll never be able to pay you back."[6]

Aware of the baggage they would be bringing to a blended family, Connie and John went through extensive premarital counseling before giving marriage a second try. Connie says, "I give God the ultimate credit for putting us together and making it work—that's number one." She calls John "the most mellow, even-tempered man I've ever met," and confesses that earlier in life, his casual approach to life might have tempted her to try to push his buttons, but no more.[7]

As for John, perhaps the best thing he has learned from his second time around is a new commitment to making marriage work. He admits that in the past, if things weren't working out in business or personal relationships, he'd just say, "Let's end it." Now, however, he says, "If I lose my job tomorrow, I have my family. That's more important than any job."[8]

Only time will tell, but I believe Connie Sellecca and John Tesh are headed for a long-lasting, happy marriage. They are a classic example of what can happen when you pair a firstborn with a last born and both partners are intelligent, perceptive, and committed to making it work.

Fred and Mary: A Different Story

There is, of course, no ironclad guarantee that a firstborn and a last born will live in wedded bliss. Mary, the permissive mother of four boys, and Fred, an autocratic father of three daughters, provide a graphic example of a controlling firstborn marrying a last born woman with a martyr life-style. Mary, who desperately needed love and approval, had always been afraid to discipline her children because she thought they would reject her. After Mary divorced and became a single mom, this lack of discipline only grew worse. There was, of course, a martyr's payoff when people would look at her difficult life and comment, "Mary, I don't see *how* you do it!" But when she married Fred, a dyed-in-the-rules authoritarian, sparks flew in a hurry.

I told Fred, "As long as you come on so strong, Mary will only defend her cubs." Fortunately, he was willing to make a real effort to practice tongue control and quit trying to improve everyone in his new family.

It was only when Fred backed off of his perfectionistic desire to control everyone that Mary was able to move toward a better approach to disciplining all the children in the family. They made slow progress, inhibited for the most part by little Peter, Mary's last born terror who needed loving but firm discipline in the worst way.

Fred and Mary were a good example of a firstborn/last born combination that was out of balance. Coming back to the teeter-totter illustration, when one teeter-totter partner is a lot heavier than the other, you can shift the fulcrum to a different point and rebalance things. In the same way, Fred and Mary had to learn to make some shifts in their approach to parenting and start working more in tandem rather than against each other. (We'll hear more from Fred and Mary and how they learned to deal with little Peter the Powerful in chapter 9.)

Additional Tips for Firstborn/Last Born Couples

Here are some other tips to help firstborns and last borns make a naturally good blend even better.

1. *If inclined to fault finding, the firstborn should back off on finding the last born's flaws.* At the same time, the last born should not flaunt his flaws in the firstborn's face.

2. *The last born can teach his or her firstborn mate to hang loose and give in now and then.* In social situations, for example, when someone is late and the firstborn begins to pace the floor like a Siberian tiger, the last born can point out that a few minutes aren't going to mean the end of the world. Last borns may also be able to model for their children and spouses a generous spirit in contributing—at church or to welfares and charities. (On the other hand, babies have to watch themselves because they can give without considering future needs

and responsibilities and wind up behind the eight ball for being too generous.)

3. *Last borns should always realize that others need their share of the spotlight.* Because last borns are carrot seekers ("Look, I'm performing, toss me a carrot"), they sometimes forget that their firstborn mates need attention and praise, too.

4. *Firstborns and last borns can take advantage of the fact that they make a great team in the game of life.* For example, the firstborn can usually size things up better and help the last born learn to grasp the big picture and realize the impact of the schedules and activities that bring pressure on the family. The last born, who is normally more of a people person, can lead the way in dealing with the feelings and emotions that circulate through the family because of conflicts that keep things from working out for everyone.

5. *Last borns can always help their firstborn mates lighten up, particularly on the kids.* Last borns, as a rule, bring the gift of fun and humor to the blended family.

Middle + Middle = Too Much Middle Ground

Ironically, two middle children can have trouble in their marriage because they do not communicate. I say *ironically* because middle children are well-known for being great negotiators and mediators, something they learned out of necessity while growing up. Somehow, though, when they marry and start building their own families, they find it easier to keep things to themselves. Either they feel it isn't worth the hassle to confront each other, or in typical middle child fashion, they discount their own opinions.

This was precisely the problem facing the all middle child marriage of George and Dorene (whom we met in chapter 5), but most of the unwillingness to confront was Dorene's, not George's. In George's case, his weakness was being *too good* at peacemaking. He tended to overlook problems rather than perceive what was happening and move to solve them. That's why Dorene's only child, Zack, was getting such a bad time from George's three kids, Tommy, Timmy, and Jane.

An effective yet very simple tool that helped George and Dorene communicate better was a *suggestion bowl*. I advised them to get a clear bowl, like a fish bowl, and put it in a prominent spot that both of them would walk by often while they were at home. They also needed pencils and different colored pads of paper for each spouse; in this case, pink for her and blue for him. When Dorene wanted to tell George something, she penciled him a quick note on a pink slip of paper and dropped it in the bowl. George did the same, writing on blue paper.

At first, George balked at the suggestion bowl, calling it "a ridiculous crutch," but I asked him to give it some time. "The reason we advise using a suggestion bowl," I pointed out, "is that some people, for whatever reason, simply cannot look their mates in the eye and tell them what is really on their mind."

As is usually the case, the suggestion bowl worked very well. Dorene was able to let off some of the steam she built up as she watched Zack get the short end of the stick on weekends when George's children came to visit. And once George got the hang of it, he became much more perceptive about what was going on in the family. Soon George was writing more notes than Dorene, also making suggestions about how they could improve relationships between his kids and Zack.

More Tips for Middle Child/Middle Child Marriages

Other tips to help middle children married to middle children have something besides a middle-of-the-road marriage include:

1. *Do your best to build up each other's self-esteem.* Let your spouse know that you appreciate his or her strengths and abilities.

2. *Give each other plenty of space for outside friendships.* Because middle children are usually big on friends and social acquaintances, it's a good idea to encourage each other to have these kinds of contacts. At the same time, both of you should take care to keep friends in the "same sex" category. Most counselors' files, including mine, have many examples of affairs that started because a husband or wife had a "special friend" of the opposite sex.

3. *Always try to do something special for each other.* If you're a typical middle child, your perception may well be that no one did many special things for you while growing up. Now that you're married, you can have empathy for your middle child mate and try to make up for lost time to help him or her feel special. Remember, your something special doesn't have to cost much or take a lot of time: a single rose for her, a bottle of cologne or after-shave for him. Or, she can tuck a little note in his lunch and he might leave her a little love note where she would find it during the day (more on this in chapter 8).

4. *Don't forget that nothing is more important to a middle child than respect.* Go out of your way to show

each other *mutual* respect, no matter what the situation might be.

Middle Child + Baby = a Pretty Good Match

When you put the middle child, typically strong in negotiating and compromising, with the socially outgoing last born, you usually come up with a healthy marriage. In fact, middle children and last borns are the third best pairing, according to birth order studies.

A plus in the marriage of a middle child and a last born is that there is a high probability for good communication—the ability to share feelings and roll with the punches. That may sound contradictory to what I said earlier about middle children tending to clam up and not share emotions, but as birth order matches go, a baby would not be as threatening to a middle child as a firstborn, so the odds for good communication are better.

There are no guarantees, of course. A lot depends on the way the last born and the middle child have responded to the environment their birth orders placed them in. Brian, born third—smack in the middle of five children—was fortunate to marry a very capable last born in Nancy, who, though she was a baby princess, turned out to be more stable, dependable, and achieving than her two older brothers.

As I chatted with Brian and Nancy after a seminar, I learned that the variable of sex had played a big role in her development as a child. She was, hands down, the "special child" in her family because, as much as Nancy's mom loved her two sons, she desperately wanted a girl. So did Nancy's dad, for that matter. When Nancy was born, it was a special event, indeed. Keep in mind, also, that although she was the baby, Nancy was the firstborn *girl* in the family.

Another major factor in Nancy's development was that her parents, both perfectionistic firstborns, had started out being very authoritarian in their parenting style. They cracked down on Frank, their older son, as well as Robert, their second born, but when Nancy came along, they eased off quite a bit and became a lot more balanced in mixing love with limits. This was a big plus for Nancy, but it didn't help her brothers too much.

By the time Nancy came along, Frank's and Robert's life-styles were pretty well formed, and neither recovered from the early authoritarian training. They excused their lackadaisical approach to life by saying, "Well, it's almost impossible to please our folks, anyway, so why bother? Besides, they were tough on us, but now they let Nancy get away with murder."

The result was that Nancy became the real achiever in the family, mixing her natural people skills with some firstborn daughter characteristics that made her exceptionally organized and dependable for a baby of the family.

When Nancy's first husband was killed in a car accident, leaving her with two small children, she approached her single mother role with the same easygoing but capable life-style she had developed while growing up. When she met Brian, a bachelor and a middle child, she got a husband with a lot of firstborn characteristics, because of how the birth order variable of spacing had worked in his life. The third of five children, Brian was born five years after his older brother, Samuel, and eight years after his firstborn sister, Sara, who was very nurturing and protective toward him during his formative years.

In effect, however, Brian was the start of a "second

family," in which he was the firstborn boy, to be followed quickly by two younger brothers. Brian wound up being the responsible one in this subgroup, earning good grades at school and becoming a compliant child who always wanted to please. Not surprisingly, he became a teacher, a natural choice for someone with firstborn characteristics.

When Brian met Nancy, he found an almost perfect match. Their individual firstborn traits didn't clash as much as they meshed, while their basic birth orders of middle child and last born brought excellent communication skills to their blended family.

More Tips for Middle Child/Last Born Marriages

1. *If you are a middle child mate, make good use of your tendency to want to "work things out."* That should blend well with your last born spouse's willingness to "talk it through." Be careful not to be condescending, however, because last borns can smell that in a minute. People have been writing them off in a condescending way for a long time, and their antennae can detect the tiniest slight or put-down.

2. *Work at blending your social interests with your mate's desire to be on the go.* If you're like most middle children, friends are important and you enjoy having people over for dinner and other social gatherings. If your last born mate is typical, he will always be ready for adventure, travel, seeing new places, and meeting new people. But be aware that the daily tensions (battles) of a blended family may put a crimp in getaway plans, much to your spouse's chagrin. If opportunity ever does knock for getting away, don't hesitate. At the very least,

grant in fantasy that which isn't possible in reality at the moment: "Honey, I'd love to go with you to that bed and breakfast, and we will, as soon as the kids settle down a little."

3. *If you're a last born, be brave enough to admit you probably have a selfish streak and a desire to hog the spotlight.* Try to cut your middle born mate some slack and back off now and then with your demands for service or attention. Remember, most middle children grow up feeling anything but special while many last borns grow up being pampered all the time. As the last born in the marriage, anything you can do to make your middle child mate feel a little pampered for a change will go a long way, particularly if your spouse is a stepdad who is struggling with surly stepchildren.

4. *Don't have fun at your middle child spouse's expense.* Last borns with the typical propensity for having fun may enjoy humor of all kinds, from practical jokes to sarcastic little digs just to get a laugh. Keep in mind, however, that if your spouse is like most middle children, she may be battling feelings of inferiority, and it can be all too easy to press the wrong button. So, when you're having fun, make a point to not do it at your mate's expense. She'll love you all the more for it.

Last Born + Last Born = Chaos

The marriage of a last born and a last born is not considered one of the better bets for success, and there is a certain amount of irony in this fact. After all, aren't last borns supposed to be so sociable and communicative? That's true, but they need to bounce off the older birth orders to keep them in line, organized, and aware that bills come due about every thirty days.

The big problem with last born plus last born is answering the question, "Who is running the ship?" When you have two last borns beginning a blended family, both bringing children to the mix, you have all their problems compounded to the power of five or six—or whatever number of kids wind up in this newly blended family. With their natural tendencies to be disorganized and irresponsible, most last borns just aren't equipped to fight back against the pressures of a blended family. They tend to freeze or just decide, "Let's have a good time and not worry about tomorrow."

(Remember, I'm not saying *all* last born/last born combinations would be ill equipped to deal with a blended family; I am saying that as a rule, last borns are least equipped for this kind of challenge.)

To cope with blended family responsibilities, last born couples need to be clear on the division of labor. In other words, they need to carefully parcel out who is going to be doing what, or they can become overwhelmed in a hurry with responsibilities, pressures, and tensions.

So, two last borns must put their heads together and decide: Who is paying the bills? Who will do the family shopping? Who will cook and clean up? Who will take charge of the social calendar? Who will clean house? Who will be "point guard" when it comes to disciplining the kids? In the matter of discipline, it's not that one parent will plan to do nothing, but both of them need to agree on *how* they plan to apply discipline (or, perhaps, *if* they plan to apply it).

If last borns don't make some firm decisions about the practical side of life, they are headed for big-time trouble. You see, babies of the family have a tendency to forget. They say, "Oh, was I supposed to gas up the car?" They also have a tendency to pass the buck and blame someone else. In a marriage, no one is a handier target than your spouse. The only problem is, if your spouse is a last born, too, guess who's catching the buck and passing it right back into your face?

Last Borns Fall into the Zigzag Syndrome

Have you ever watched someone trying to row a boat when he doesn't have a clue about how to operate the oars? He's all over the lake or going in circles because he doesn't know how to pull those oars and make them work to keep the boat on course. So it is with many last born marriages—what I sometimes call the *zigzag syndrome*. When two last borns hook up, they don't really understand how to pull together, and the result is zigging, zagging, and running in circles, possibly spiraling down to disaster.

The zigzag syndrome had Trevor and Jill going in circles when they finally decided they needed counseling. A friend recommended me to them, and they agreed to give counseling a try—which, in itself, was fortunate, because last borns are not famous for admitting they need professional help. By far, the majority of my clients have been only children, firstborns, and, to a lesser extent, middle children. Babies just don't think they need counseling; besides, they don't have time because they're having too much fun.

But the fun had turned sour for Trevor and Jill for several reasons. Money problems were a big reason for the failure of their first marriages, but they hadn't learned their lessons. Totally committed to a "play now and pay later" plan, they had tried to extend their dating days right into the first eighteen months of their new marriage. They both carried checkbooks for a single account, which they drained with abandon when they weren't abusing their credit cards. Each expected the other to "keep things straight," and, of course, that never happened.

The bank was constantly sending notices of overdrafts, and Trevor or Jill frequently had to rush over to cover the bounced checks. On top of that, they had been "lucky" enough to assume the mortgage on a beautiful new home that the owner was willing to let go at a huge loss because he had been transferred out of state and simply had to have whatever cash he could scrape together. With a low down payment, Trevor and Jill moved into a house that they simply couldn't handle financially, even though both of them had jobs. They justified it, however, on the grounds they needed the room for their four kids—his two and her two.

Actually, helping them understand their financial insanity was the easy part. They were willing to stop using their credit cards, and we had a little ceremony as I cut them into small pieces and handed them back saying, "No more credit cards for the foreseeable future." Then I got them in touch with a local nonprofit agency which specialized in rescuing people just like Trevor and Jill from the financial swamp.

But even with their finances headed for a better footing, there was still a lot of tension between Trevor and Jill. Their financial woes were only a symptom of their real problem, which had its genesis in their ingrained habit of passing the buck and blaming each other for what went wrong. I recognized this rather quickly because, you see, "it takes one to know one." All my last born life I have battled this same propensity. The tendency to overspend is something else I've struggled with—or should I say, my wife has struggled with my tendency more heroically than I have. Fortunately, Kevin the Cub married firstborn Sande, who keeps him somewhat in line.

An acute example of how Trevor and Jill tended to blame each other for their problems turned up when they told me about recently letting go of a major responsibility they had taken on at their church. Just a few months after their wedding, they had decided to become youth sponsors, which put them in charge of about forty-five teenagers, ages fourteen to seventeen. With four kids of their own under twelve, this decision wasn't very wise. When you have a blended family, all of your resources need to be geared to making that blended family work. Outside commitments are not a very good idea, but Trevor and Jill took on the job because they agreed that it sounded like such fun—being able to help teens and, of course, join them on socials and outings.

Predictably, however, they were soon taking a lot of heat from angry parents who kept calling with "suggestions" on how to improve things. And they were getting plenty of complaints from Trevor's sons, Mike and Nick, as well as Jill's daughters, Sharon and Constance, who all wanted to know, "When do you ever spend any time with *us?*"

Although they had agreed to be sponsors for at least a year, they dropped the youth group after serving for only six months. This left the pastor, not to mention the youth director, rather perturbed, and they both let Trevor and Jill know that they had let everyone down. Naturally, that put both of them on a guilt trip, and in typical last-born fashion, they blamed each other for what had happened.

"It's all your fault," Jill said tearfully in one of our

sessions. "I really wanted to stay, but you got mad and called the church and told them we were quitting."

"What are you talking about?" Trevor fired back. "I only did it because you were crying and carrying on after Mrs. Hamilton called and chewed you out. I thought enough was enough. Besides, you didn't have time to be a good mother. I only did it for you!"

And so it went. It took several sessions for Trevor and Jill to see that their ingrained tendencies as last borns clearly pointed them in the direction of forgetting their responsibilities, not following through, and then passing the buck when things got tough. Still smarting from being told she didn't have time to be a good mother, Jill was pleased when I straightened Trevor out on his need to take more time to be a good father.

On the plus side, however, I was able to use some of their positive traits to put the marriage on better ground. Both Trevor and Jill were people persons, and they were willing to talk. They weren't always that skilled at listening, but eventually they worked through their problems and got some answers.

Tips for the Last Born/Last Born Couple

1. *Two last borns must be aware that they can be quite manipulative by nature.* The result is that they play games with one another, often selectively hearing only what they want to hear. Later, when called to account, they respond with, "Oh, I didn't understand it that way *at all* . . . I never really agreed to do *that* . . . Why didn't you *tell me* that's what you wanted? I had no idea!"

Two last borns must vow to shoot straight with each other, but not *at* one another. Once Jill and Trevor recognized how they manipulated each other with selective listening, they were able to work on tuning into each other's real wavelength, and their relationship improved a great deal. Strangely enough, they had an easier time with their budget, too.

2. *Learn to be active listeners.* A simple technique last borns can use to cure selective hearing is *active listening*. This means you listen with more than just your ears. You look directly at your partner and try to sense your partner's feelings as well as whatever facts are being communicated. I sat Trevor and Jill down in chairs directly opposite each other so that their knees practically touched. I even had them hold hands and then talk about their problems. The rule was that, while one person spoke, the other could not interrupt, and before replying the listener had to "feed back" to the speaker everything that he thought he had heard.

If you're thinking this is a ponderous way to have a discussion, you are right. But strangely enough, taking time to do it now and then does help both participants realize that they're not always hearing what the other is saying, much less understanding the meaning. (We'll look more closely at how to use active listening as a parent in Part 3.)

3. *Hold each other accountable.* To go along with their newly acquired skill of active listening, I also taught Trevor and Jill to hold each other accountable for their actions. If you're a last born married to a last born in a blended family, you may want to try this simple plan: Sit down at least once or twice a week and ask each other some pointed questions. "How are we doing on the budget?" "Is the checkbook under control?" "Are the kids under control?" "Have you talked to your son about beating up my daughter?" "Have you talked to your

daughter about being more respectful to her stepdad?"

As you hold each other accountable, be sure to use active listening and avoid being defensive. Avoiding defensiveness may not be easy for two last borns who chafe under the pressures of a blended family, but use the positive skills that came with your birth order: your laid-back approach to life and your ability to handle people and stay loose in a crisis. Remember, as a baby of the family, you "earned a living" by looking up and learning how to get around all the older kids and other insurmountable problems. You'll be able to get around your blended family problems, too, as you work together. Oh, yes, one other tip:

4. *Keep that last born sense of humor and never give up*. Never, never, never!

Birth Order Is an Arrow, Not the Answer

Now that I have given you the "best" and the "not so good" birth order combinations for a marriage, are you encouraged or discouraged? Suppose, like Rita and Wally, you are a firstborn married to a firstborn. To make matters worse, one of you is a controller and the other is a pleaser. Or, perhaps, like Fred and Mary, you and your spouse are a supposedly perfect blend of a firstborn and last born, except for one thing. You are not getting along at all!

If your birth order cards are stacked against you, or if you don't fit the typical profile, what should you do? Bail out of the blender as soon as you can? Obviously, the answer to that question is no. Birth order is only an indicator that points you in certain basic directions. What *you* do with your birth order—and your life-style and life theme—determines how you will come out in a blended family, or any family, for that matter.

The point is this: Whatever your birth order and that of your spouse, it's what you make of your particular birth order strengths and how you modify and deal with your particular birth order weaknesses that will decide what kind of marriage you will have. That's why love must be a lot wiser—and stronger—the second time around. One of the best ways to make it strong is to learn to speak each other's love language. We will learn how to do that in the next chapter.

NOTES

1. See Walter Toman, *Family Constellation* (New York: Springer Publishing Co., Inc., 1976). Toman studied 3,000 families before coming up with his conclusions. In a smaller study, Dr. Theodore D. Kempler, University of Wisconsin, researched 256 business executives and their wives and also discovered that certain birth order combinations made better marriages than others. The smaller study is documented in Lucille Forer's book, *The Birth Order Factor* (New York: David McKay Co., Inc., 1976), 187–88.

2. Kevin Leman, *The Birth Order Connection* (Fleming H. Revell Co., 2nd edition, 2001).

3. See James 3:3–4.

4. Toman, *Family Constellation*.

5. Bob Thomas, "Connie and John: Lessons in Love," *Good Housekeeping*, March 1994, 128.

6. Thomas, 129.

7. Thomas, 129.

8. Thomas, 129.

CHAPTER 8

Men Are Microwaves, Women Are Crock-Pots

One of the major principles I try to communicate to couples who come to me when their marriage starts getting bumpy is this:

Respect the way your partner sees life.

It sounds simple enough, but for some reason it's not. Perhaps it's a lot harder than it looks because seeing behind your partner's eyes involves *discovering* your partner's needs and then being willing to try to *meet* them. Meeting each other's needs is difficult enough in a first marriage, but in a second or third marriage it becomes even harder. Why? Because the partners are so busy trying to cope with all the needs of the children in their newly blended family, it's too easy to overlook the most important needs of all—*their own.*

And why are the needs of the husband and wife the most important in a blended family? What about all the children that have been brought together, all of their pain, hurt, anger, guilt, and other baggage? They are important—very important—but I still maintain that your needs and your mate's are absolutely primary. That's because you can make a stable, organized, loving home for the children in your blended family *only* when you have a strong, stable marriage relationship.

Be aware; in fact, *beware:* The typical stepfamily is a mortal enemy of a second marriage. Your kids (and your spouse's) will be out to test your relationship and, in many cases, they may even try to destroy it. Those are strong words, and you may be thinking, *Leman is exaggerating—again.*

I wish I were. You may be one of the lucky ones who is living in a stepfamily without ever getting stepped on; if so, you are rare. The facts are that in the typical stepfamily, the new marriage stands as a reminder to all the children of the failure of two other marriages that came before. As one blended family mom told me, "When you remarry and you both have kids, you aren't just a mom and a dad. Now you're a father and a *stepmother,* a mother and a *stepfather.* The kids never let you forget that."

Exactly. Blended family children have had to give up their biological nuclear family for something that, in their minds at least, is second best—a binuclear stepfamily. It doesn't matter that their first family was full of tension, stress, arguing, fighting, or abuse. In their minds, it was *their home,* where Mom and Dad lived with them. Even if one parent, or possibly both, did not treat the children all that well, it doesn't matter. To paraphrase the old cliché: Blood is always thickest.

Many couples realize all this when they get married— at least, they tell me they do. They understand that the children will not necessarily be that pleased. They are aware, in some cases, that the children will be downright hostile. Nevertheless, the couple is sure that they can make it work, that they can achieve the ideal of a healthy blended family. But in most stepfamilies, this ideal never becomes reality. Some stepparents and stepchildren never do blend. Perhaps they reach a state of polite truce, or maybe they develop a measure of respect for each other. But there is never a bonding equal to that between the biological parent and child.

That's okay. In fact, it's a good idea to accept that bonding with your stepchild is a nice ideal but probably won't be reality. But what you must try to do with every tool and weapon at your disposal is to bond with your spouse and make your marriage as strong and impregnable as possible. Only then will you be able to withstand the testing and probing, the poking, prying, and chipping that your kids will do to see if the two of you are "for real."

And if they find they can't break you down, a strange thing usually happens. They feel more secure and settle down to blend into the family as well as they can.

But, if you and your partner want to stay strong enough not to crack under the relentless pressure that the kids will apply, you have to understand each other's needs, and to understand each other's needs, first you have to understand your differences.

Men and Women Are Different—Very Different

It used to be fashionable to insist that men and women were not different. But most people were always aware of the obvious: men and women are not the same.

For instance, the typical man's need to control has

been well documented. Rather than ask directions, he'd rather drive forty-five miles out of the way (or around the same block eight times) and "find it himself." For one other obvious example, modern man doesn't even have to leave his recliner for total control. Just put a TV remote control in his hand and he's in hog heaven. Or put it in someone else's hands and watch him squirm.

On the other hand, women have their own peculiarities. For example, they prefer to answer the call of nature in coveys—up to five or six at a time—as they leave together to "go freshen up." Men, of course, wouldn't be caught dead saying, "Hey, Joe, Harry, and Frank— let's all go hit the john."

Even with all the advancements that have been made in the '80s and '90s, men still aren't known for being very sensitive. Watch women interact in any social setting and you will quite likely hear them talking about feelings. And what are the men doing? They are over in the corner making fact oriented observations about everything from the latest political scandal to who's going to win the pennant.

When a man meets a man in a public setting—on an airliner for example—the first question is usually, "And what do you do for a living?" Men prefer to flash their vocational badges. Work is a safe subject they can handle without having to become too open. But women, by nature, are more transparent and live much closer to their feelings and emotions. Two women may meet for the first time and in fifteen minutes they're telling each other their life stories.

While most men seem to have little trouble making up their minds, women tend to go back and forth on decisions, sometimes indefinitely. In a restaurant it's typical for a woman to study (memorize?) the menu, check all the specials, and see if she can try something new. When with a group, she may be heard to say, "I'll wait until everybody else orders, *then* I'll decide." Or, she may look over at the next table and say longingly, "I wonder if *that's* really good."

You see, when a woman goes into a restaurant, she wants to enjoy the *entire* experience—the ambiance, the table decorations, and, of course, the wonderful choice of foods. If the menu offered a "sampler plate" that allowed her to take a bite of this and a bite of that—and that and that and that—she would probably order it. The typical man, however, is not interested in ambiance—he wants *food*. If he has been to the restaurant before, he has usually decided what he's going to order before he ever enters the place. You may have overheard, or participated in, a scene like the following:

She: "What are you going to get, dear?"

He: "Steak—I feel like a good steak."

She: "Why don't you order the pasta along with the steak?"

He: "I don't like pasta."

She: "But if you order it, I can have a bite."

He: "If you want pasta, why don't you order it?"

She: "Oh, no, that's too much to eat. I'm just getting a salad, and all I want is a bite of pasta."

Now I realize that the examples I just cited leave me leading with my chin with some feminists who would be quick to charge me with chauvinist stereotyping. After all, there are men who go back and forth on what they want, and there are men who are willing to share their feelings. True enough. But as I share these observations on the differences between the sexes while speaking to thousands of couples in various settings, I get an immediate "I've been there" response, from women as well as men.

There is a lot of discussion today about how women are changing. Recently I saw an article about women hiring other women to do their housework. They might have to skimp on groceries, but they are absolutely determined to have the housecleaning service come on a regular basis. "Cleaning services are booming," wrote the female author, "a trend that is expected to continue into the next decade, as women struggling to have it all are deciding they don't have to do it all."[1]

"Changes" like this are quite evident, and they're getting major coverage in magazines and on TV talk shows, but I believe these are superficial issues. On the surface, women seem to be changing, but their *basic needs* remain the same.

What Does She Really Want?/What Does He Really Want?

A lot of men, especially, ask, "What does she really want?" Baffled husbands will sometimes plead with me to give them the answer. I tell them I'm not sure what a woman *wants,* but after listening to several thousand of them behind closed counseling doors, I have a fairly good idea of what a woman *needs.* We counselors have different ways of describing human need, and I try to keep my list short. Admittedly, my list isn't as short as that of one husband I counseled.

When I asked him, "Do you know what your wife's greatest need is?" he looked blank for a moment and then replied, "VISA?"

I never did figure out if he was joking or serious. As

important as those little pieces of plastic are to most modern marriages, I believe that when all of the complaints, longings, and feelings are shaken down, a wife really needs three things:

- *Affection:* "Just hold me, hug me; we can undress later."
- *A stable family:* "Be committed to me—and my kids . . . yes, even until death do us part!"
- *Conversation:* "Let's talk; let's be interested in and understand each other."

As for men, what I hear them saying about their needs is this:

- *Sexual fulfillment:* "Make love with me because you want to, not because you have to. And sometimes it would be fun if you came on to me *first!*"
- *Companionship:* "Be my best friend."
- *Respect:* "Recognize the role I play in this family. I'm out there busting my tail for you and the kids!"

Which Birth Order Is Best at Meeting Needs?

Getting behind a partner's eyes is downright difficult for just about everyone, but it's harder for some birth orders than for others. If you're guessing firstborns and only children have the most difficult time, you're right. They're so busy making plans, reaching goals, toeing the line, trying to be perfect, conscientious, trustworthy, punctual, organized, and in control that they fail to see (perhaps I should say they fail to *really look at*) their partner's needs. More compliant firstborns or controllers who have learned to give as well as take, however, can learn how to be more sensitive to a partner's needs over time.

Before moving along, we shouldn't neglect to mention that special breed of super firstborns—the only child. The only child spouse will have many of the firstborn traits mentioned above, but added to their problems will be difficulty in grasping why the kids are always squabbling. The typical only child spouse will complain to his mate, "I don't understand it. Why do they have to fight?"

Why, indeed? The only child doesn't have a clue because he never had any brothers or sisters to fight *with*. When he discovers his children or her children or all the children duking it out, he relies solely on logic and tells squabbling siblings and stepsiblings, "Well, if you can't get along, then just don't play with each other."

Never having been in the position of having to share with or get along with siblings himself, he has no clue as to how or why the kids seem to be able to keep the war raging on and on.

The bottom line is that the needs of his children, and probably his spouse, will probably go overlooked because the only child husband is so frustrated with the madhouse in which he finds himself.

Next come the last borns, the self-centered babies who are so busy having a good time that they tend to ignore the needs of others because they're concentrating so much on their own needs. Once I can get a last born focused on her partner's needs, however, it's a different story because then the last born can bring her people-person skills to bear and improve things a great deal.

Probably the best at recognizing a partner's needs is

the middle child—the one person who knows what it's like to have needs neglected or ignored. But even the middle child faces problems because he or she may have retreated into a cocoon of nonconfrontation, where it's a lot safer to operate. Bring the middle child out where he or she can comfortably confront, however, and you have the most empathic of the birth orders.

What Is This Thing Called Commitment?

There is a great deal of talk today about commitment. Women keep complaining that they can't find men who are willing to commit. That's why their need for a stable family is so crucial.

After counseling thousands of couples and being married myself for over twenty-seven years, it is my opinion that the best foundation for a marriage commitment is a spiritual foundation—a shared faith in something or Someone far greater than you are. Frankly, I do not see how any couple can make it without a common faith. While I never push my own Christian beliefs on any client, I especially urge married couples to find a church where they can both attend and to make regular worship a part of their lives.

And when it comes to a blended family, the need for a spiritual foundation is far greater. Living in a stepfamily means getting stepped on, at least now and then. When your spouse or your children or, more than likely, your stepchildren are trampling your feelings or failing to understand, being able to go to a loving God who cares is a source of power that is irreplaceable. Repeatedly, I have had clients tell me how a spiritual foundation has been the absolute salvation of their marriage.

"Let me put it this way," Barbara said. "It would never have gone off as well as it has without the Lord in our lives. It never would have. I know that's a cliché, but I don't know how people can successfully blend a family without God. I just don't see how it's possible."

Melissa told me, "Number one, I wouldn't expect anyone to go into a stepfamily without the Lord ahead of them, a shared relationship with the Lord. That's just kind of a given."

"Having a common faith can make or break it in a blended family," Alan declared. "If you don't have God there, I don't see how you're going to make it."

With a shared faith, a couple is in a better position to make a decision (maybe a better word is *determination*) to stand together no matter what. When a couple shares spiritual values and has a common faith, they are bound together in a way that makes it very difficult for children or anyone else to drive a wedge between them.

How Is Love Expressed at Your House?

There is a great deal of teaching that suggests marriage is supposed to be strictly a giving proposition. A spouse is instructed to unconditionally love and accept his or her mate without necessarily receiving anything in return. This seems to be a beautiful ideal, but it falls far short of reality, and it's my opinion it falls far short of what God really intends marriage to be.

If marriage is a union of a man and a woman into "one flesh," it follows that one part of that union cannot be doing all the giving while the other part is doing all the taking. Some couples try to use a *quid pro quo* arrangement—"If you do this, I'll do that." That's an improvement on one partner doing all the giving while the other one does all the taking (a sure ticket to divorce court), but it's far from the best arrangement.

Real love finds one partner giving one hundred percent to the other and, in turn, the other partner gives one hundred percent back. There must be a give and a take, an ebb and flow to marriage, or each partner's "love tank" will empty in a hurry.

Like many marriage counselors, I believe that in each of us is a reservoir, put there by our Creator to store the love we receive from others. Human beings cannot live without love, and surely a marriage will die if each spouse's love tank isn't kept reasonably full.

A book I recommend highly for married couples is *The Five Love Languages* by Dr. Gary Chapman. His theory is simple. Each spouse must learn the partner's primary love language in order to be an effective communicator of love. According to Chapman, the five love languages that keep your partner's love tank full are:

1. *Words of affirmation*. These include verbally complimenting, encouraging, reassuring, cheering up, congratulating, or honoring your mate.

2. *Quality time*. This involves giving your spouse undivided attention, usually in conversation, as you express feelings and listen for them as well.

3. *Gift giving and receiving*. These gifts should be tangible or visible expressions of love. They don't have to be expensive, but enough thought should go into them so that they truly please your spouse.

4. *Acts of service*. In a marriage, acts of service include anything that needs doing around the house, particularly the mundane, boring, and even dirty jobs that are always there.

5. *Physical touch*. This runs the gamut from acts of affection that might be as simple as touching each other as you walk by, to hugging, back rubs, kissing, and sexual foreplay leading to intercourse.[2]

It doesn't take a rocket scientist to figure out that as you speak the five love languages you will be meeting basic needs—for a wife: affection, family stability, and conversation; for a husband: sexual fulfillment, companionship, and respect.

Can Microwaves and Crock-Pots Coexist?

The obsession of the typical male with sex is well-known. Many men, myself included, will say that by far and away the most important need for a husband is sexual fulfillment. There is, by the way, a big difference between sexual fulfillment and having sex. I certainly enjoy sex, but the fulfillment comes in knowing my wife enjoys it as well and that we actually connect in a deeply spiritual way.

Unfortunately, many a husband's sexual needs go unmet (or not met often enough) because he isn't meeting needs in his wife like affection and conversation; they aren't communicating. One of the most frequent complaints I hear from husbands is "She is just not interested in sex anymore." And from the woman's side, the most frequent complaint is: "Sex, sex, sex, that's all he wants—can't we ever just cuddle?" (I'm not saying, by the way, that women are sexless, or that they don't like sex or need sex. Nor am I saying that men don't really want to be affectionate. What I am saying is that with the typical married couple, the wife is more interested in affection, the man more focused on sexual fulfillment.)

I like what counselor and author Gary Smalley often says about men, women, and sex: When it comes to being ready for lovemaking, men are like microwaves and women are like Crock-Pots. Easily stimulated by their own imaginations, not to mention the sight of female curves, men are ready in seconds for the sexual act.

Even in this Information Age, it is amazing how many men don't seem to understand that women take longer to warm up. They don't recognize the need for hugging, other forms of affection, and communicating with their wives with affirming words. Yet, these are the time-tested ways to let a woman know she's desirable, important, and really loved and cared for. This is what turns her on and makes her ready for sex.

Be Aware of the Half-Mile Rule

It's a funny thing about women and sex—they just have to be in the right frame of mind. Chuck Swindoll, nationally known pastor and best-selling author, was our guest on "Parent Talk" one day, and I commented, "Chuck, my wife subscribes to the half-mile rule."

"Half-mile rule? What's that?" Chuck asked, taking the bait completely.

"That means," I explained, "we can't have sex if there is someone within a half mile of the house."

That's an exaggeration, of course, but it's true that women need the right atmosphere before they are "in the mood." And most men don't understand that because it's not that way for them.

On the other side of the coin, most women don't really understand a man's deep need for sex. Many of the remarried couples I counsel are in a blended family because there was a tremendous misunderstanding about affection and sex in their prior marriages. And now the same problems are cropping up again. She says, "All he wants is sex." He says, "She doesn't want to make love, she just calls me an animal."

Many couples are on a no-affection-no-sex merry-go-round. When a woman doesn't get enough affection from her husband, she will either shut off sex completely or engage in it with a "lie there like a log" attitude. I've talked to many a husband who tells me he's sick and tired of being told, verbally or nonverbally, "Just pull my nightie down when you're through."

Of course, when the woman withholds sex or participates with all the enthusiasm of a turkey the week before Thanksgiving, she simply shoots herself in the foot, so to speak, because this is not the way to get affection from her sex-starved husband.

In *His Needs, Her Needs,* another excellent book that I highly recommend for married couples, Dr. Willard Harley sums it up perfectly:

> *When it comes to sex and affection, you can't have one without the other.*[3]

Women Like a Slow, Creative Hand

While there is no magic formula for solving the no-sex-no-affection merry-go-round, husbands can always try some obvious things that have worked ever since Adam looked at Eve and said: "Wow! This is *it!*"[4]

For example, husbands need to ask themselves how affectionate they are being toward their wives. If they were to be scored on an affection scale, with 10 being best, where would they rate? What specifically do they do to show affection toward their wives? When considering this last question, men should be aware that grabbing breasts or genitals is *not* a show of affection; actually, it is a guaranteed way to irritate a woman who hasn't been stimulated and made ready for sexual contact.

And that leads to another question: Does the husband know the difference between foreplay and just satisfying his urges? With all of the information that is available today on sexual technique, you would be amazed at how many men, including those who have already been through one ruined marriage, don't understand the importance of certain critical areas of the female anatomy like the clitoris.

I have counseled many husbands who fall into a distinct pattern. Usually they are firstborn controllers who have very regimented occupations—such as engineers, draftsmen, or accountants—but any birth order could be guilty. Their wives are very unhappy with a lot of things, especially the same predictable approach to sex at the same predictable time. I try to explain to this kind of man that he must loosen up a little and get creative. Making love to his wife is not an engineering project, and his wife is not always going to be the same.

Every time he gets into bed with his wife, he really has a different woman on his hands, in a sense, because women are much more apt to like one thing one day and something else the next. I try to get the calculating controller to try different things—rubbing her feet, her back, her neck. Then and only then can he start to work up to kissing, caressing, and fondling more interesting areas, but never should he grab or hurry. Don't be guilty of what Josephine said about Napoleon's approach to sex: He went at it "like a fireman tackling a fire."[5] The once popular song is all too true: Women want a man with a slow hand and an easy touch.

She Needs Conversation, He Needs Companionship

When I say *conversation* is a vital female need, I mean women want something more than merely talking together. This "something more" is *communication,* which, unfortunately, has become a cliché in marriage counseling literature. Cliché or not, communication, or the lack thereof, is still a frequent reason people give for getting a divorce. Running a marriage without communication is like running an engine without oil. Sooner or later, the engine self-destructs.

Maybe a better term for communication is *conversational chemistry.* Without it, the remarried couple trying to blend a family is severely handicapped. With all those birth orders bouncing off one another and all those lifestyles crossing and clashing, there is just too much emotional input that has to be processed each day. There are too many feelings that need sorting out, too many opinions that need to be acknowledged and accepted, too many misunderstandings and misconceptions that need to be set right.

Again, a key factor that must be considered here is *time.* It takes time to converse and to learn how your wife really feels. Men are notorious for being willing to settle for the facts and being seldom tuned into feelings. In the blended family, especially, emotions are running high and the wife has a lot of them. If you don't think so, just ask any stepmother who has had "another one of those days" with stepchildren who have given her gas emotionally and would like to do so literally if they had the chance!

A crucial male need that correlates somewhat with the woman's need for conversation is companionship. In *His Needs, Her Needs,* Willard Harley talks about men needing "recreational compatibility."[6] This doesn't mean that a wife has to fish, hunt, or rock climb. Ideally, it's best if you can find an activity that both of you like. Harley lists over one hundred activities that husbands and wives can consider to find things they like to do together.[7]

It helps, too, if each of you is willing to give a little and join your spouse in something that isn't necessarily your favorite pastime. Giving a little worked well for Sande and me. I am the consummate University of Arizona sports fan, with season tickets to all Wildcat football and basketball games. And Sande is usually right there with me, although she really doesn't care that much about sports. She doesn't *hate* watching, but sometimes I find her busily knitting or even looking through a recipe book just when the Cats are on the three yard line, poised for the winning touchdown.

Sande, on the other hand, has always been a lover of antiques. There was a time when I couldn't care less about antiques, but it's interesting how things can change.

We spend our summers in western New York State, which seems to be full of old antique shops located on dusty back roads. Rather than let Sande venture off alone, I preferred enjoying her company while she pursued her odd hobby (odd to me, anyway). At first, I stayed out in the car while she went into the antique shop to browse. But sitting in a car on a hot sticky New York summer day is no fun, so eventually I started moseying into some of these places, which often looked like something out of an Alfred Hitchcock movie. At times I fully expected Norman Bates to leap out at me with a big knife (an antique knife, of course).

But then a strange thing happened. Antiques became interesting. Eventually, I started to *like* antiques. Now, when we go for those drives on dusty back roads in upstate New York on hot summer afternoons and we spot an antique store, we race to see who can get out of the car the quickest to find the first "treasure" of the day!

She Needs Stability; He Needs Respect

By now it's possible that an obvious question may have occurred to you: "Are the needs for a person in a first marriage the same as they are for a person in a second or third marriage?" For the most part, there is no difference, *except* the woman's need for a stable family. In a blended family, for many women, this basic need suddenly leaps right to the top of the list. Many women who remarry are looking for a commitment to family that just wasn't there the first time around.

I have talked to many wives who got remarried to a certain man because "he looked like he'd be a good father to my children." While it is true that the marriage comes first, any man in a blended family should realize that showing love and affection for his wife and showing love and affection for her children (his stepchildren) are practically one and the same.

I will even go as far as to say that the wife in a blended family will love her husband to the degree that she knows her kids are okay. In fact, as a husband focuses on making sure his wife feels safe about having her kids around him, the way is then open to meeting her needs for affection and conversation.

Also, stepfathers must realize that parenting takes time—a *lot* of time. Most women already know this, but men tend to be more vocation oriented. They are, therefore, sometimes oblivious to the fact and need to be reminded. Willard Harley recommends that men and women try to spend fifteen hours a week together in doing mutually enjoyable recreational activities, and he adds to that *another* fifteen hours a week as a goal for quality family time where everyone is involved.[8] Does this sound too idealistic? Maybe, but it is a target well worth shooting at if you want to make your blended family work.

While the most keenly felt need for husbands, bar none, is sex, a close second is respect. Men never want to admit it, but preserving their delicate male egos is very important.

This is especially true in a blended family. I've talked with many a stepfather who was baffled by his stepchildren's hostility or by their total lack of respect for anything he had to say. And quite often his wife is siding with her children, sometimes inadvertently, perhaps; but nonetheless, she is leaving her husband feeling as if he's out in the cold, shut off from the very people he is trying to blend with.

If the wife wants to score points with her blended family partner, she should seriously consider the fact that men have fragile self-images. The legendary delicate male ego is all too real. Men often look supremely confident, as if they have it together, but inside they may be coming apart. Many normally perceptive wives don't seem to grasp this. I've seen it again and again in my office: the wife criticizes the husband or complains about him. If I suggest that encouraging him might get better results, she looks at me incredulously.

Another tip for wives who want to show respect to their husbands is not to share intimate or private details of their married lives with friends or family members. A man seems to be funny that way. He really doesn't appreciate having a mother-in-law or sister-in-law come up to him and say, "I heard you think Samantha doesn't need a new Easter dress," or "What's this about you being chewed out at work? What's going on?"

On the other hand, if a husband wants his wife to show him respect, along with admiration and encouragement, he needs to demonstrate the characteristics and qualities that will motivate her to do so. For example, he can show her proper affection and take time to communicate with her in genuine conversation that rises above, "Wow, I had a rough day! What's for dinner?" As he meets her needs and gives her the feelings of security that she desperately seeks, she can't help but show him the respect and admiration that he so desperately seeks in turn.

One of the most encouraging examples of how this works was Ruth, who had divorced her first husband after five years of listening to his verbal abuse and grieving over his total neglect of their two boys, Ben and Casey. Her second husband, Howard, had not been married before. A firstborn, he had grown up in a very large family and had been responsible for several younger siblings. When he met Ruth, he had instant rapport with her two young sons, who responded to his affectionate hugs and "wrestling matches" with enthusiasm.

"I loved Howard's affectionate ways," Ruth said. "And

he loved that I was such a good mom. So we were a great pair from the start."

When I asked Ruth what her greatest challenge was in blending her family, she said, "Trying to accept all the attention and the love and the kindness from Howard. That was the hardest part for Ben and Casey and me—just accepting all that attention, because we just weren't used to it."

Dear Kevin, I Like It When You . . .

To help husbands break the needs impasse (you meet my needs and then I might meet yours), I often try to explain how a man can make love to his wife without setting foot in the bedroom.

In counseling or in a seminar, I often tell the story of the time I asked Sande, "Honey, would you make me a list of things that I do, or could do more often, that make me a better husband?"

"Sure, I'll be glad to," Sande said, and, in true first-born fashion, she whipped out a little spiral notebook and began scribbling suggestions with the same speed she makes out a grocery list. To be truthful, I thought she might put down two or three ideas, but she came up with a dozen "Honey-Do's" in no time!

For seminars I've reduced her list to ten, and I share it below. In each case I comment on the love languages being spoken when I do what she describes.

1. *Whenever I'm sick, take the kids to church anyway.* This act of service is important to Sande, especially because of her strong Baptist background.

2. *I like it when you scratch and rub my back to wake me up in the morning and then bring me coffee.* Here

we have physical touch combined with a small act of service in the bargain.

3. *I like it when you help with the dishes and pick up around the house, when you see what needs to be taken care of and you take care of it without me having to point it out.* Sande seems to be focused on acts of service—is there a pattern here?

4. *I also like it when you don't call attention to what you're doing to help.* Sande tells me that rattling the empty coffee cups to let her know that I'm taking them to the sink doesn't impress her. And, of course, she has listed another act of service. I think we have definitely found a trend, and it's not too hard to see why. Sande is a firstborn pleaser and she likes it when people, especially her husband, do things to please her for a change.

5. *I love it when you say, "You need a weekend away. I've made arrangements for you to spend some time alone."* To that Sande added that she always likes it when I take care of the kids while she's gone instead of dumping them off at my mother's or at a baby-sitter's. Here we have an act of service *and* the giving of a gift. Sande needs her space, and over the years I've often invested in sending her off alone where she can just relax without the constant pressure of family demands.

Recently, I dropped her off at a nice local hotel on Sunday after church. After checking in, she relaxed by the pool with a book I bought her—one I knew she wanted to read. She had the whole afternoon and evening to read, relax, suntan, and sleep—her favorite sport. Meanwhile, I spent the day and the evening playing Mr. Mom with our two little girls, Hannah, seven, and Lauren, two.

The next day, after Sande slept in and had a leisurely breakfast, I picked her up following a late check-out and brought her back to reality, refreshed and recharged. Oh, yes—for those who are curious—I did clean up the kitchen. I even made the beds!

6. *I also really appreciate it when you do things for my mother.* Yes, acts of service for mothers-in-law also pay off. These include providing her with transportation and helping her get things fixed around the house.

7. *I like it when you take care of my car.* Sande enjoys this practical act of service. Regularly, I get her car washed and serviced so she is sure it's safe to drive.

8. *You don't know how much I appreciate it on those days when I'm at the end of my rope with the children and you take over when they really get wild and start arguing with each other.* Here I am again in the service of my spouse, but I'm also giving her words of affirmation and my time as well. When I take time to help my pleaser wife at the end of a day she has spent pleasing everyone else, it says "I love you" in great big letters.

9. *I like it when you make the plans for us to go out.* In other words, I get the baby-sitter, I call up our friends, and I set a time to meet them—so nothing is left for Sande except to get ready. Granted, all this planning ahead is tough on a baby of the family, but I'm at Sande's service because I know that's her favorite love language.

10. *I love it when you're patient and understanding—especially if I've had a bad day.* Along with being a pleaser, Sande is an organized, capable firstborn, and words of affirmation are always helpful when the day hasn't gone as planned. At times like these, any or all of the love languages can come into play as the following story will illustrate.

In a postscript to her tenth point, Sande reminded me of the time she drove the van through the garage door. The kids were waiting when I walked in. Obviously, I had seen the door already, and they clamored, "Dad, Dad, what are you going to *do* to her?"

I went out to the kitchen where Sande was chopping up carrots, whacking away on a big cutting board with a *very* big knife. I knew it was time to speak love in all five languages. She needed my words of affirmation. She needed quality time, with my undivided attention. She needed a gift. She needed an act of service, and she needed a hug, which I gave her as I asked, "How was your day, Honey?"

Choking back a sob, Sande said into my shoulder, "Oh, *fine!*" And then I said, "Let's go out to dinner."

Sande was so pleased and relieved, she didn't even want to take time to repair her makeup. We bundled all the kids into the van, which had suffered some minor dents and scratches as well as the loss of its luggage carrier, and headed for our favorite family restaurant. As we stopped for a red light, Sande sighed and muttered, "Kevin, I can't believe I *did* that."

I suppose it was time for more tender words of affirmation, but the mischievous Cub could not resist: "Oh, Honey, I don't know . . . I can sort of believe you did *that.*"

The kids howled with glee from the back seat, and I stole a glance at Sande. Would Mama Bear laugh or start crying again?

For a half block or so, she didn't say anything, but as we turned into the restaurant driveway, she turned to me and said, "Do you think I should have the Denver omelette for dinner or the cashew chicken salad?"

Mama Bear had nicely ignored my little dig, which everyone knew was just for fun, but I think the kids still learned something from what happened that day. They had often heard me say, "Hey, when the milk spills, you get a rag." And now they were learning that when the van goes through the garage door, you call State Farm.

Dear Sande, I Like It When You . . .

And, for the ladies, I also have suggestions on how to make love to your husband—in and out of the bedroom. Just for fun, I worked up my own "ten ways you can love me best" list and gave it to Sande.

1. *Arrange for us to go out alone.* You may have noticed that Sande also put down this same act of service, which also leads to having time together. It's really not too hard to understand why. As a couple, we've spent over twenty years in the daily minutiae of raising five kids who divide into two families. We had our older three, Holly, Krissy, and Kevin II well into high school when all of a sudden along came Hannah, and then five years later, Lauren arrived. So we both like it when the other realizes, "Hey, it's been a few days since we've been alone." And that's why we're both willing to make the effort to set something up.

I'm sure many wives are wondering, "Who arranges the time to go out alone the most?" We are pretty much fifty/fifty on that one—one more indicator of how the firstborn Mama Bear balances nicely with her last born Cub!

2. *Surprise me at work.* I call this a gift, or maybe *serendipity* is a better word. Sande calls ahead and talks to my secretary to be sure the calendar is clear for lunch, or maybe there is a "window" in the afternoon schedule for a leisurely coffee break. Then she "just happens" to drop by to say hi, and we're off to spend some time together. For a variation of that, Sande will call the office and, if I'm free, she will come on the line to ask me how

my day is going, or share the newest adventure or the latest accomplishment of one of the littler Lemans.

3. *Kidnap me for an "overnight."* The gift of time I like most is having Sande surprise me by arranging for child care, picking me up after work, and announcing we're headed for Phoenix, only an hour and a half up the freeway. Once there we spend some time shopping—at some of Sande's favorite stores—have a nice dinner, and then check in at a nice hotel for the night. The following morning, after a leisurely breakfast, we drive back home.

4. *Tuck a card or a love note in my briefcase.* When I'm on a trip, I love to find these words of affirmation from Sande. Sometimes she finds a clever greeting card and puts in her own special note. Other times, it's something she's scribbled hurriedly on a slip of plain white paper, telling me that she loves me, that she'll be praying for me, or that she knows that I will do well on a talk show or at a speaking engagement.

5. *Give me a little gift for no particular reason.* Gift giving is always great love language for a last born. It doesn't have to be expensive, it just has to be a gift—a tie, soap-on-a-rope, or maybe a golf shirt. Because I'm color-blind, Sande frequently buys me clothes. She still remembers the time when, left on my own, I brought home two shirts—one chartreuse and the other a garish orchid. I thought they were nice shades of yellow and blue!

6. *Pay me compliments of any kind, in front of others or when we're alone.* I'm not particular, I love words of affirmation in the form of compliments. Again, I guess I'm simply a typical baby of the family who loves his strokes and recognition. If there is an audience, so much the better!

7. *Come up behind me, hug me, and kiss the back of my neck.* This act of physical touch is usually a favorite with most males of any birth order. I know it is with me because if I play my cards right, it might lead to another of my favorites—her joining me in the shower. Environmentalists should note that my only motivation for sharing the shower is to save our precious water supply here in the parched deserts of Tucson!

8. *Cuddle with me in the Jacuzzi and talk.* This is another way that Sande gives me the gift of time—conversation and words of affirmation. It's our version of recapping the day, or the week, as we share what's been happening. Granted, we're giving to one another, but I put it down as something I especially enjoy. When Sande helps me talk through problems, I know that she respects and supports me. I appreciate how she patiently listens to me complain about how it is out there in the big, bad world.

9. *Say to the children, "Not now, I'm talking to Daddy."* These are words of affirmation, indeed! It's Sande's way of saying she respects me and she doesn't always want to focus on her children, as precious as they are. This, by the way, is an excellent way for a remarried woman to speak love language to her spouse, who may think that she's more interested in her children than she is in him.

10. *Keep me informed because I hate to hear something important from a third party.* This communication is another act of respect that I would put under words of affirmation. Do we see a pattern forming here for a baby of the family who was often "written off" while growing up? But in the blended family especially, it's a wise wife who doesn't forget to tell her husband about important phone calls, arrangements she has made that

affect everyone's schedule, and other "mundane" details that can drive a man crazy if he is left in the dark.

As a postscript to my Big Ten list, here is one more practical reason why the man's need for respect runs a close second to sex. Many men in stepfamilies tell me they feel as if they are being used. They are just "meal tickets" who are supposed to provide the money for bills and other expenses. A husband can easily wind up feeling exploited when his stepchildren barely grunt "Hello," even though their stepdad is paying to keep them in private schools.

Any little act of respect, paid by his wife, can help salve the wounds. Sometimes it's fun to mix respect with a gift containing words of loving affirmation. I treasure a CD Sande gave me that features Celine Dion singing "The Power of Love." I especially like the line that says, "I am your lady . . . you are my man!" I may be fifty-something, but my response to that is, *"All right!"*

Go Ahead, Try This at Home

Now that you have some models to work with, you may want to try this "I love it when you . . ." exercise at home. I suggest that each of you fill out ten (or maybe you'd settle for even five or six) ways you'd like your mate to say "I love you." Exchange lists and talk about what each of you has said. Then decide which kind of love language each request or comment suggests.

Whatever you do, focus on each other, not the kids. Spend this time strengthening the most important element of your blended family—your marriage. You will get to the kids in due time, and so will I—coming up next in Part 3.

NOTES

1. Nancy Imperiale, "Maid Service Is Growing As Women Decide It's Okay To Hire Someone to Clean House," *The Arizona Daily Star,* March 18, 1994, D–1.

2. See Gary Chapman, *The Five Love Languages* (Chicago: Northfield Publishing, 1992), chapters 4–8.

3. Willard F. Harley, *His Needs, Her Needs* (Old Tappan, NJ: Fleming H. Revell Co., 1986), 39.

4. See Genesis 2:21–23, *The Living Bible Paraphrase* (Wheaton: Tyndale House Publishers, Inc., 1971).

5. See Jane Goodsell, *Not a Good Word About Anybody* (New York: Ballantine Books, a Division of Random House, Inc., 1988), 64.

6. See Willard Harley, *His Needs, Her Needs,* chapter 6.

7. Harley, 79–80.

8. Harley, 83–84, 141–42.

PART THREE

Putting the Pieces Together

A Tactical Plan for Blending Your Family

CHAPTER 9

The Seven Secrets of Blended Family Discipline

The proud owner of the brand new twenty-one-foot day cruiser hadn't sailed the waters around Buffalo and Grand Island much before, but Lake Erie was choppy so he decided to head down the Niagara River and show his lady friend some of his navigating skills.

The west branch of the Niagara provided some idyllic scenery, and then, as they headed on north past Navy Island, he decided to cut the engine and just drift with the current so that they could enjoy the scenery. As they came around a bend, he wasn't sure but he thought he saw rapids up ahead—and was that *mist* in the distance?

Just then, a siren shrieked to the starboard, and he looked up to see a Coast Guard patrol boat bearing down on him at high speed. As the long arm of the law came alongside, a bullhorn bellowed, "DO YOU HAVE ENGINE TROUBLE?"

"No, not really," the weekend admiral shouted back. "We were just drifting for a ways to enjoy the scenery."

"MAN, DO YOU KNOW WHERE YOU *ARE?*"

"Not exactly. I think we just came out of the West Niagara River."

"THAT'S RIGHT, AND ABOUT A MILE FROM HERE YOU WOULD HAVE GONE RIGHT OVER NIAGARA FALLS."

"Thhhaanks for the warning," the day cruiser owner managed. "We're out of here!" He hit the throttle and was out of sight in seconds, no doubt a shaken but wiser man.

I know this scene may sound a little farfetched, but, unfortunately, it's reenacted many times each year when unknowing boaters wander too close to the danger zone above Niagara Falls. As I grew up in the Buffalo area, I often heard about boats that had wandered too far down the river and gotten into real trouble.

Are You Drifting Toward the Falls?

As I have counseled hundreds of families, original and blended, I've sometimes thought of those boats drifting downstream, headed unknowingly for Niagara Falls. Parents often come to me because their children are totally out of control and they are at the end of their rope. When I inquire about what system of discipline they use to cope, I often get the feeling they are adrift with no real plan in mind. The approach they are using is obviously not working, and unless somebody sounds the siren, they are headed for real disaster.

You have probably heard some child-rearing expert comment: "People are required to take a course to learn how to drive; they are required to take a course to learn how to give CPR; but *anyone* can become a parent with no credentials whatsoever." Without training or input, most people tend to parent the way they were parented.

When they marry—or remarry—they bring the same parenting style they grew up with, which in most cases means either authoritarianism or permissiveness or a mixture of both.

Permissiveness is based on a warped idea of love: "All we have to do is *love* little Buford and everything will be just fine."

Authoritarianism is based on a warped idea of limits—the more limits the better: "As long as you live under *our* roof, you had better toe the mark, *or else*."

It's not uncommon for one parent to be basically permissive while the other's style is authoritarian. In other cases, one parent may use both styles, depending on how the parent feels at the moment. Usually the parent tries to be "nice" and is permissive to a point. Then, when little Festus builds a fire in the living room without the benefit of a fireplace, the parent goes ballistic and cracks down with authoritarian wrath.

Swinging back and forth—from permissiveness to authoritarianism and then back again—is an inconsistent approach that treats the child like a yo-yo. It's no wonder that so many children grow up to become yo-yos who have a terrible self-concept and practically zero self-esteem. When they marry and become parents themselves, they may be aware that what they're doing isn't working, but it's not easy to kick the habit.

One blended family mom, a firstborn, told me she has a hard time because she's constantly fighting her own reactions to the parenting style she learned from her father. As we talked, she told me of an incident when her five year old, also a firstborn, was throwing a temper tantrum and she couldn't get him to calm down. Naturally, her son is the one most like her, so when she sees him out of control, it really gets to her.

She got so frustrated she screamed, "You want something to cry about? I'll give you something to cry about!"

And the very moment she said those words, she could see her dad's face right there in front of her. "I see all this coming out," she told me, "and then I try to fight it, but I'm left with, '*Now* what do I do?'"

This mom's plaintive question is a good example of why parents need a system of discipline that achieves a happy medium, where the children get plenty of love but also some reasonable limits that teach them how to be accountable and responsible. This need is especially acute in the blended family, where a couple seeking to blend her kids and his must present a united front.

According to many stepfamily specialists, discipline of the children is the number one issue in the blended family. I agree. As I emphasized earlier, you and your spouse will stand or fall, sink or swim, *together,* and if there is anything the two of you need to work through and agree upon it's, "Who will discipline the kids and how will it be done?"

As you work out a system that you both can be comfortable with, a good rule of thumb for blended families is:

> *Start out with each parent disciplining*
> *his or her own natural children.*

In the majority of cases I've seen, natural mothers need this rule more than natural fathers do. The natural mom is reluctant to let the stepfather discipline her kids. If she has been living for some time as a single mom, it's not unusual for her to have slipped into a permissive approach, and she may be reluctant to do much disciplining, period. In other cases, however, the natural dad may be the one who is lax, and he will tend to leave the disciplining to his new wife, a practice which often places her in the role of the wicked stepmother.

So to begin with, in the blended family it is best if natural parents handle the disciplining of their own children. This should be a short-term solution, however, and in the long run, you want to find a system where both of you can discipline all the children consistently and lovingly.

Stepparents should work into disciplining their stepchildren a little bit at a time. Don't leave all the disciplining to the natural parent because this will undermine the stepparent's position of authority in the home. I have talked to many stepfathers, in particular, who feel emasculated because they "don't dare say anything" to stepchildren. But at the same time, their wives are reluctant to let them do any disciplining because they think they will go too far.

The Seven Secrets of Loving Discipline

In any family, the key to discipline is finding the right balance between giving the children plenty of *love* and giving them adequate *limits* that hold them accountable for their actions. In the blended family, this problem is multiplied because suddenly, children and adults are brought together in a stepparent/stepchild relationship. They have no history, no bonds have formed, no trust has been developed.

Blended family parents need a system that can help them bridge these gaps. They don't necessarily need to institute law and order, but they do need to use "love and order."

Principles of discipline that I have taught consistently

are described in a book I wrote over ten years ago, *Making Children Mind Without Losing Yours.*[1] For blended families, I call this system *Loving Discipline* because it gives you a consistent, decisive, respectful approach to disciplining your children and assuring them of your love at the same time.

Maintaining this delicate balance in a blended family is vital because you are dealing with children who have been "ripped" and deeply hurt by divorce (or the death of a parent). They need compassionate guidance and training plus the limits that make them feel secure and stable. All parents need to walk the line between authoritarianism and permissiveness, but blended family parents need to walk it with special care as they practice the following principles:

1. *Relationships come before rules.* All of the secrets of Loving Discipline must be used *gently* but firmly in order to obtain the best results. If parents in a stepfamily try to use Loving Discipline without extra sensitivity to the anger their children feel (usually because of the divorce that made their blended family possible), its effectiveness will be greatly reduced (more on anger in chapter 10).

2. *The whole is more important than the parts.* With all those birth orders and life-styles bumping and crisscrossing, certain family members may try to control the entire family. When Loving Discipline is practiced consistently, all family members are treated fairly; all get equal time and equal opportunity to participate and contribute.

3. *You are in healthy authority over your kids.* In other words, you are not too authoritarian or too permissive. You strike a middle ground that some parenting specialists call *authoritative*. In the blended family, the

crucial question is, "How much healthy authority can the stepparent exert with his or her stepchildren?"

4. *Hold children accountable for their actions.* Loving Discipline does not *punish* but lets the child pay a reasonable consequence for misbehavior or a poor attitude. In a blended family, goals and rules must be carefully spelled out. Clearly communicate as well *who* holds whom accountable.

5. *Let reality be the teacher.* Using reasonable consequences as a tool and not a weapon in the blended family is an art. When telling a blended family child, "I'm sorry, you broke the rule, and now you can't go to your Little League game," you must be sure to temper firmness with friendly good humor.

6. *Use action, not words.* A key to Loving Discipline is to give children responsibilities, but always reserve the right to "pull the rug out." Try to avoid prescribing punishment ("If you do *this,* then *that* will happen"). Make clear the kind of behavior you expect from your children, but keep the consequences varied, depending on the kind of training you believe they need at the moment. This keeps them a bit off balance, but it helps them concentrate on being responsible and accountable instead of simply trying to avoid certain predictable consequences.

7. *Stick to your guns.* This is an all-important principle, particularly when a child is wailing, crying, carrying-on, or telling a stepparent, "You're not my father!" In a blended family especially, sticking to one's guns does not mean mowing everyone down. It means being firm in enforcing whatever rules you all have agreed upon, even when your heart is breaking for the child who has just chosen to lose an entire weekend of wonderful activities by not being responsible.

And how do these secrets of Loving Discipline work

in a blended family where parents may be poles apart on how to discipline the children? Let's look at some real life examples.

Fred and Mary vs. Peter the Powerful

Discipline was a major issue in the home of Fred and Mary, whom you met back in chapter 4. Fred was the father of three girls who visited only on weekends and during the summer, and Mary had custody of her four boys, who, to put it kindly, were "running wild," particularly five-year-old Peter.

Here's a second look at Fred and Mary's family structure.

Fred (firstborn authoritarian controller)	Mary (last born permissive martyr)
Jami—11	Jeremy—12
Judy—9	Brad—10
Becky—6	Mark—7
	Peter—5

Fred and Mary were one of the most extreme cases of an authoritarian marrying a permissive that I have ever counseled. When they first came to see me, they cited problems with their marriage, but it didn't take many sessions to see that one of their key problems was the discipline (actually, the nondiscipline) of their children.

A big reason why Mary's first marriage had failed was her extremely permissive approach to raising her four sons. With the life-style of a martyr ("I only count when I suffer"), Mary thought that the only way she could keep the loyalty and devotion of her boys was to give them nothing but love. Her first husband had finally gotten fed up and left.

Because martyrs are often attracted to powerful controller types, it was no mystery why Mary decided to try marriage again with Fred, a big, handsome, assertive man who gave the impression of always being in control of the situation. In his first marriage, however, Fred had chosen a firstborn who wasn't about to be controlled. She was anything but a pleaser, and they had clashed continually until she finally decided she'd had enough. She had obtained custody of their three daughters, who lived with her but came to see Fred on weekends and during the summer.

When Fred married Mary, he immediately saw that her four boys needed some discipline. But when he clumsily tried to use his assumed authority, he ran smack into a den of badgers. Fred had succeeded in alienating Mary and all of her boys, who went out of their way to let him know he wasn't their father and they didn't really have to do what he said. Because Fred's life theme was "I only count when I'm running things well," he constantly swung from frustration to livid anger.

Mary was very protective of all of her cubs, particularly five-year-old Peter, whose destructive antics had not only his older brothers ready to kill him but his three stepsisters as well. And, whenever Fred gave him an order or even a suggestion about anything, he ran crying to his mother.

Peter Finally Went Too Far

The straw that helped bring Fred and Mary's discipline problems out in the open was the day that Mary had stepped next door to take something to a neighbor and little Peter decided to put Puff, the family cat, in the clothes dryer. Fortunately, just then Fred arrived home from work, and he heard the poor beast thumping and squalling in the dryer. Fred rescued Puff just in time, but as he reached in to remove the dazed and frightened cat from his revolving prison, he was severely bitten and scratched. Shocked and enraged, Fred took little Peter over his knee and paddled him soundly.

It was the first spanking Peter ever received, and Mary came back home just as Fred was applying the final swat. When Peter saw his mother, he ran howling to her side and hung onto her leg for dear life. Still angry, Fred tried to explain how Peter almost murdered the family cat, but Mary would not listen. They ate dinner in total silence, and Fred spent the night on the couch.

The next day, when they came in for their regular appointment, Mary angrily described Fred's "barbaric" treatment of her son and said she was just about ready to leave the marriage. Fred was still frustrated and angry, but he did not want to lose his wife and blended family. He added, however, that he felt most of the situation was Mary's problem, and if she'd only let him take charge he could have her four sons "shaped up in no time."

I could see I had a selling job to do with Fred and Mary to get them to start using a balanced system of Loving Discipline. I suggested to Mary that I talk to Fred first, in private. From past sessions, I was well aware that Fred was not only a controller, but he was a very *conservative* controller who put up with no nonsense.

As I tried to sell Fred on the secrets of loving but not punitive discipline, I pointed out that a man with his take-charge style needed to use his head and not just follow his feelings. Fred's desire for discipline and order was good, but his approach was simply setting up power struggles in his family, I told him.

"If Mary's boys are afraid of you, they won't approach you, and you can be of little help to her in controlling them," I pointed out. "They'll just continue to push her buttons. You know Mary's a pleaser; she wants everybody to be happy, so when the kids come up to her teary-eyed, what's she going to do?"

"She goes along with the kids every time," said Fred with a sigh.

"Exactly. You can help Mary get into healthy authority over her kids, but you've got to do it with a little different style."

"A little different style?" Fred pondered. "Which means what?"

"For one thing, it's obvious that you haven't been asking your four stepsons what they think; you simply have told them what you have decided. They have had no say, and so they drag their feet or set their heels, or go running to Mom for protection, and she charges to the rescue. In a blended family like yours, Mary has to feel that her boys are safe with you, and right now she's convinced they're not. In fact, maybe the first person you should ask, 'What do you think?' is *Mary*. When you tell Mary what the kids should or shouldn't do, it only makes her more defensive."

Fred pondered my words carefully. Stopping to ask, "What do *you* think?" would be a big step for him. Up until now, he had been asking all the wrong questions: "*Why* did you do that?" "*Where* have you been?" "*How* could you say that to your brother?"

When I took Mary aside to talk to her in private, I knew that the key to making any progress with her was in appealing to how we were going to *help her kids*.

With her martyr's mentality, this is what Mary would want to know.

"Mary, I realize that you feel bad about a lot of things—the divorce, the way the boys were hurt, the scars they'll have for life. You're trying to protect them from more hurt, but I think you'll admit that things are getting out of hand. I know you want to be a good mom, and the best way you can do that is to provide your kids with some structure."

"That's what Fred is always talking about," Mary said apprehensively, "structure and being more disciplined. He doesn't know the boys the way I do, and he just comes on too strong."

"I've talked to Fred, and he realizes that," I assured her. "At the same time, I think you'll have to admit that you are sometimes *too* loving. Now if the two of you could use the best of each of your strengths, you could give the boys the loving discipline that they actually really want. I'm sure that's one reason why they're acting out as much as they do—particularly little Peter."

Did Peter Just Need a Good Spanking?

Fred and Mary left my office with a lot to think about. Fred had agreed to spend the next week working at taking the edge off of his voice and to stop asking the boys "Why?" whenever they irritated him. Mary hadn't leaped enthusiastically at my suggestion of Loving Discipline. She had lived in her martyr's fantasy world so long that the word *discipline* didn't really sound that attractive at the moment. She had agreed, however, that the boys were definitely out of control and that something needed to happen.

During their next session, Fred and Mary listened intently as I explained and illustrated my Seven Secrets of Loving Discipline, continually emphasizing that love without limits left children feeling insecure and much more inclined to powerful behavior. But, I added, limits without love crushed a child's spirit.

As I went through the Seven Secrets, Fred seemed to have few problems. He kept nodding assent, especially when I mentioned being in "healthy authority over the children," and "taking action to pull the rug out."

I cautioned Fred, however, by explaining, "Mary needs to approach parenting with more firmness, but you need to back off and use your strength and power judiciously. Being in healthy authority means coming on strong enough, but never in a punitive way. Loving Discipline is not punishment; it is caring for your children and respecting them as you hold them accountable for their behavior."

"Okay, I hear what you're saying, doctor," Fred replied, "but just how can we start using your system?"

"Well, right now, Mary thinks you are Genghis Khan, and you have to give her your word that you're going to be gentle in applying discipline."

I looked at Mary, and she only nodded, swallowing hard. I went on. "If both of you will give this a try, I know you will find a balance that will provide the kids with the stability that they are really longing for. And if you get a few wins under your belt and the kids see that things are going to be different around the house, they'll respond favorably."

"But how can we deal with Peter?" Mary wanted to know. "He's only five . . ."

That Mary was even willing to consider dealing with Peter was a breakthrough. It seemed that the cat he had put in the dryer was Mary's favorite, and she was at the end of her rope with him—for once. Also, the more I talked about mixing love with discipline, the more I could see her becoming convinced that perhaps she could make a stand with her children without their rejecting her.

"I'm glad you mentioned Peter," I said. "He has been acting up to get attention and be important, so much so that he's disrupting the family. But if you continue to let little Peter get away with murder, that just antagonizes and infuriates the other children, and they won't want to cooperate at all. Loving Discipline says the whole is always more important than the parts. As you start giving him some Loving Discipline, the older children will see that little Peter the Powerful is going to be dealt with, and they'll become more amenable to discipline themselves."

"I'm willing to try to work something out," Mary said slowly, "but it's going to be hard. I just don't like to see anyone else trying to discipline my kids, particularly since I haven't been very much into discipline anyway. I think the hardest part about your system will be holding the children accountable and having them pay 'reasonable consequences.' Does that mean spanking? I really don't want Fred paddling my boys again—I couldn't stand it."

"Spanking—or what I like to call giving the child swats—is really a last resort," I assured Mary. "I know a lot of the experts say spanking is wrong, but I think that properly done, spanking can help when a fairly young child like Peter is being absolutely defiant and will not listen. As for your older boys, they will be much more responsive to the withdrawal of privileges, having to pay for things they break or misuse out of their own allowance, and any other kinds of reasonable consequences."

"I don't think I could ever spank Peter," Mary said. "I don't think I have it in me."

"That's for you to decide, Mary," I replied. "My guidelines for spanking are pretty basic. It never means whaling the daylights out of a kid. You do it when you're under control. You spank only when the child is being absolutely defiant and is putting himself in danger or totally disrupting the family. Two or three good swats is usually all you need with a small child to get his attention. And then it's very important that you always pick the child up, hold, and stroke him and reassure him that you love him very much. That is absolutely the most important part."

"Dr. Leman," Fred interjected, "let me ask you something. If Peter were your child instead of ours, would you spank him?"

"Let me put it this way. Little Peter's saddlebags are packed full of power and they need to be deflated just a little bit. A good way to get his attention and convince him that things are going to be different could be giving him a swat or two. I assure you, this will not damage his little psyche for life."

"The way you describe spanking doesn't make it sound that bad," Mary admitted, "but I think I'd prefer to use some kind of withdrawal of privileges or some other kind of consequences as a general rule."

"That's fine. It's your call, Mary, and you must make the decision. Peter's old enough to understand a reasonable consequence such as losing a privilege for misbehavior," I said. "Just remember, every situation is a little different, and it will depend on what the misbehavior is and what you feel is at stake. The important thing is that you work everything out with Fred and have him backing you all the way. You admit you've never been a disciplinarian and you'll need him for backup if you're going to establish any kind of loving discipline that really changes things."

It wasn't easy, but Fred and Mary managed to work together to make some specific plans on how they would approach the children. Fortunately, they had several positives going for them, including their natural firstborn/last born connection, which usually makes a good marriage. They truly loved each other and wanted to make it work, so they were able to take some first small steps toward the use of Loving Discipline.

Peter the Powerful Meets His Waterloo

One of the first things I advised them to do was to sit down and have a family conference with Mary's sons. Fred's three girls, who came only on weekends, could be talked to later.

Difficult as it was for her, Mary led the discussion. She told her boys that she loved them very much—perhaps too much—and that she had been lax in teaching them to be responsible and accountable for their actions. She said, "We're going to try something new around here, and your stepfather is going to help me. It's called Loving Discipline, and the idea is that if you break family rules or misbehave, you have to pay a consequence."

"And I want to say that I'm sorry that I got off on a bad foot with you guys," Fred chimed in. "I tried to order you around when I really didn't have the right to do so. From now on, however, I will be helping your mom enforce some rules."

"What kind of rules?" Jeremy, Mary's firstborn twelve year old, asked suspiciously.

"Well, Jeremy," Mary answered, "one rule you're going

to like, I think, is that no one in the family is to violate another person's property or go into another person's room and mess things up—that kind of thing."

Brad, the ten year old, gave Peter a hard look, and asked, "And what happens if somebody does come in my room and messes up my homework?"

"He's going to lose a privilege that he really enjoys," said Mary. "And if he keeps it up and deliberately defies me, there will be trouble."

"What kind of trouble?" asked Mark, age seven.

"Let's just leave it at *trouble,*" said Mary, setting her jaw with resolve. "Whatever happens, I'll discipline you boys, but your stepfather is going to be right there to back me up and help me. This isn't going to be easy for me, but we just can't go on the way we have."

During the entire family conference, Peter, the powerful five year old, said nothing, apparently more interested in playing with a toy car than in taking part. After dismissing her sons, Mary and Fred agreed that their first family conference had gone fairly well, but they both knew that little Peter would soon call their bluff.

It didn't take long. The very next morning, Brad let out a bellow of rage and came to Mary holding up his math homework, which was now covered by a mass of crayon scribbling. "Peter did it!" screamed Brad. "I saw him in my room, and besides, he's the only one who's ever done anything like this!"

Mary could see Peter peeking around the corner of the door with a look on his face that seemed a cross between "I wonder what you're going to do" and "I can still get away with murder if I want to."

At that moment, Fred, who hadn't left for work yet, walked in. He took one look at the ruined homework, and then he looked at Mary as if to say, "*Now* what do you do?"

As Fred told me about what happened, he said he had never seen such a determined expression on his wife's face before. She strode over, took Peter firmly by the hand and led him to the bedroom, where she applied three swift, hard swats on his ample little bottom. Then as Peter howled with pain and sobbed pitifully, she comforted him and let him know that she loved him but that he simply couldn't be ruining his brother's homework anymore.

Meanwhile, Brad had quickly passed the word to his brothers about what had happened. All the boys were impressed—even awed—by what Mom had done. When Fred's daughters arrived for their next weekend visitation, Brad, the middle child whose homework Peter had ruined, practically met them at the door and said, "Guess what? Peter got spanked! And guess who did it?"

"Oh-oh," Jami, Fred's oldest said. "Did Dad lose his temper again?"

"No," Brad replied, "it was *Mom*. We can't believe it!"

One battle never wins a war, and there were many that followed after Mary first drew a line in the sand. Family conferences with the boys, as well as with the girls when they were present, were held weekly as Mary and Fred tried to pick their way through, what seemed to them, a new mine field called Loving Discipline. Fortunately, Fred's girls had always been disciplined firmly, and except for a few birth order collisions with the boys, they were relatively little trouble when they visited on weekends. This enabled Fred and Mary to concentrate on Mary's four sons.

"Pulling the Rug" on Brad and Jeremy

Not long after Mary "pulled the rug out" on Peter for ruining Brad's homework, another showdown occurred, but this time it didn't involve the baby of the family. One of the chronic thorns in Mary's side had always been how lazy the boys were about keeping their rooms clean. In a family meeting, she and Fred got everyone to agree to a new rule: All rooms had to be cleaned by Friday night—that was the boys' responsibility and it had to be done without fail. Remembering what had happened to Peter, the older boys said, "No problem, Mom, don't worry about us."

Sure enough, the very next Friday, Mary checked Brad and Jeremy's room and found the usual disaster. Mark and Peter's room was not too bad, but this was easily explained because Mary had been giving them guidance in keeping it straightened up. She would let them do as much of the work as they could, but she was right there watching.

Brad and Jeremy, the older boys, had been left on their own, and instead of cleaning their room, they had gone their usual way to play Nintendo and catch a favorite TV program. When Mary looked at their room on Friday night after dinner, it practically qualified for Federal Disaster Aid. She didn't say a word, but the next morning at breakfast, Jeremy reminded her, "Mom, I've got to get down to Little League practice, and Brad has to get to his soccer game."

"I'm sorry, fellas, the car is not moving," Mary said firmly. "You remember the rule we all agreed upon— your room had to be clean by Friday night."

Jeremy and Brad looked at each other and dashed to their room to do a quick repair job. Ten minutes later they were back, letting Mom know that their room was now straightened up and could they go to Little League and soccer?

"I'm afraid not," Mary said kindly but sadly. "The

rule you agreed to was that the room has to be clean by Friday night, and trying to do a hurry-up job on Saturday morning does not mean you escape the penalty." Jeremy, Mary's firstborn, stormed off to his room and slammed the door. Brad stayed to plead that she knew he was a star player on his team, they *needed* him. How could she possibly keep him out of the game?

Mary wavered but stuck to her guns.

"Brad, I'm not keeping you out of the game. You kept yourself out of the game when you didn't get your room cleaned by last night. If we don't enforce the rules we have here, they won't mean anything. I'm terribly sorry. You'll just have to call your coach and tell him why you can't be there today."

When Mary and Fred reported what had happened, I commented, "That must have been hard, but there is no question that you got their attention. They had agreed to certain rules, and when they didn't follow them, you pulled the rug. You can bet that they're thinking, *We better do what we promised we'd do—Mom obviously means business.*"

Slowly, surely, and sometimes dramatically, Fred and Mary made progress in achieving healthy authority over their children. By using Fred as a sounding board, Mary was usually able to stick to her guns, even when discipline became especially hard. "Sometimes I think we're trying to change too much too fast," Mary confided in one of their last counseling sessions. "I think it's especially hard for my older boys, Jeremy and Brad, who went ten and twelve years without discipline, and all of a sudden I'm clamping down."

"Yes, but from what you've been telling me, they're responding quite well," I assured her. "It's probably hardest with Jeremy, who's gone the longest without discipline, but remember that firstborns really like order, organization, and rules. Just keep taking it slow, but always be consistent. And never forget that relationships come before rules. Your kids will appreciate rules as long as they are sure you love them and care about them."

Fred and Mary continued working together, and eventually she even started trusting him to play a more active role in disciplining her sons. The day I heard that he had handled several minor problems well while Mary was gone for the weekend to visit her mother, I knew it was time to dismiss them as clients. (My policy is to keep no one as a client for very long—three to six months is average.)

I could see that Fred and Mary were becoming a real team. They were going to make it, not only with their children, but with each other.

Loving Discipline Is a Team Sport

When spouses work as partners, one can make up for where the other may be lacking, and vice versa. Together, the parents form a powerful team that their children may test and even defy at times, but in the long run they will feel more secure because they finally understand that this marriage will last.

When one partner, however, allows the other to cope with discipline alone, everyone suffers. This was the problem with Veronica, whose two girls, Danielle and Carrie, were nine and eleven when she married Garth, the father of Cole, a seven-year-old boy. Everything went fairly well for the first two years because Cole was still in the custody of his mother, who lived out-of-state.

Garth managed to see his son about once a month, and he did his best to stay in touch because he knew his first wife had a drinking problem. The problem grew worse, however, and Cole often made frantic calls to his dad saying, "Mommy won't wake up again." Garth hired a lawyer and, after a bitter and expensive fight, was able to get custody of Cole on the grounds that his ex-wife could not provide proper care for the boy.

Veronica had managed to rear her two girls with minimum discipline problems, but when Cole arrived in their home, he soon drove her crazy. He was seldom disciplined when his mom and dad still lived together. After Garth and Heidi divorced, little Cole had been virtually on his own. As Cole's stepmother, Veronica often wound up in situations that called for disciplining Cole, but Garth was either unavailable or uninterested. When Veronica complained about Cole's behavior, Garth just shrugged and said, "I'm sure you'll figure it out."

An assertive firstborn, Veronica finally told Garth, "No, I really can't figure this out. You've got to be the disciplinarian, too. You've got to discipline this child; he's a spoiled rotten little brat!"

Garth and Veronica quarreled continually over Cole, and eventually they wound up in my office. Frustrated and teary-eyed, Veronica put her complaints on the table: "I'm basically in charge of the house. My husband's out working, and even though I've had to work, too, most of the responsibility of keeping the household running still falls on me. I can discipline my own girls, but Cole just ignores me."

Two of the biggest bones of contention were Cole's failure to do homework or any chores around the house. According to Veronica, she spent every evening hassling Cole while Garth nursed a Coors and watched *Sports Center* on ESPN.

As I listened to Garth's side of the story, I learned that

he was a middle child who had developed a noncon-frontive life-style. He worked hard all day at his job as a mill foreman, and when he got home at night he just didn't want to cope with any "kid problems." Although he appeared to be laid-back, he was a controller, none-theless, and was taking advantage of a wife who had grown up trying to please. But now that her second marriage was proving to be as frustrating and unfulfilling as the first one had been, she was getting fed up.

Obviously, Garth needed some instruction in the use of Loving Discipline with his son, Cole; but even more important, he needed to learn how to love his wife with-out setting foot in the bedroom. I had several private sessions with him in which he admitted that for the first two years, his marriage had been great. Veronica's daughters had accepted him fairly well, especially since he never bugged them about anything—he always left that to their mother. But after Cole arrived, his sex life had practically come to a halt.

"Your wife is a firstborn perfectionist who obviously could handle things back when she only had to deal with you and her two girls. But now that Cole has arrived, she's become stressed out. Is it really any mystery why your sex life has dwindled? She has to work all day, then she comes home and fights all evening with your son while you nurse a tall cool one and watch TV. By the time Veronica comes to bed, she is exhausted and about as interested in having sex as she is in cleaning the attic."

Garth was like so many husbands I have worked with: he simply had no clue about what he was really doing to his wife. He thought that what happened in their house was the way marriage was supposed to work. Fortunately, Garth was the typical middle child who wanted to stay married. He had been crushed when

Heidi had ended their marriage, preferring to lose herself in drinking. He didn't want this marriage to end as well, so he agreed to make some changes.

I told Garth that according to the principles of Loving Discipline, the whole was always more important than any of the parts, *including him*. That meant he had to start pulling his share of the load at home, and he also had to help little Cole understand that he wasn't more important than everyone else in the family either.

"Both parents need to be in healthy authority over the kids," I explained, "and in the blended family, it's best— at least at the beginning—for the natural parent to discipline his own children. Cole needs to hear from you; don't pass the buck to your wife."

"Okay, Doc, I'm willing to try," Garth replied. "What's the best approach?"

"Sit down with Cole and let him know that from now on you're very interested in seeing that he fulfills his responsibilities—his homework, taking out the trash, and anything else he has been assigned. Don't necessarily threaten him with, 'No homework, no TV or Nintendo.' You always want to be able to pull the rug and use action, not words, but not on a prescribed basis. The point is, with Loving Discipline, you want to teach the child to want to be responsible instead of always simply fearing a specific penalty if he doesn't do something."

Just as I had with Fred and Mary, I sat down with Garth and Veronica and introduced them to the Secrets of Loving Discipline. Veronica caught on immediately because she had instinctively been using a lot of these same methods. She particularly liked my advice concerning Cole's refusal to take out the trash: "Don't say anything, just let him know that it's his responsibility.

When he doesn't fulfill that responsibility, simply hire one of his stepsisters and pay her out of his allowance just once. You'll be amazed at how quickly Cole will decide that taking out the trash isn't such a bad deal after all."

Garth and Veronica started working together to apply Loving Discipline. Naturally, Cole tested his dad to see if he meant business, and Garth struggled to be firm but loving at the same time. With Veronica's help, he got the hang of it, however, and while Cole didn't become an *A* student, he at least brought his grades up to average. As for the trash, I was right. Cole only needed to see his sisters get paid out of his allowance just once. After that, the trash was always out on time.

And with my urging, Garth started to spend more time with his son—they began taking in some baseball and football games together. Best of all, however, Garth started spending more time with his wife, listening to her and talking about how to blend their family more effectively. Not surprisingly, Garth's love life improved immeasurably.

Use Different Approaches to Different Birth Orders

Some good general rules for using Loving Discipline are:

1. Be fair.

2. Be consistent.

3. Treat each child differently.

One reason not to treat all your children the same is that each birth order responds to discipline in a different way.

When dealing with a firstborn of any age, be sure everyone knows the rules. Firstborns want to know exactly what is required of them, what is right and *fair*. Taking a little time to spell things out for your firstborn will pay off in many ways. This will show him that you respect him and care about him. At the same time, it gives you a better lever for using Loving Discipline.

When a firstborn does break the rules or misbehaves in some way, sit down with him and ask, "Okay, what were the rules on this one?"

For example, suppose your firstborn ten year old takes a plate of spaghetti, piled with rich, red marinara sauce, into the family room, and as he tries to sit down and watch TV at the same time, the whole thing lands on your nice, new peach-colored carpet. After having him help you get the mess out of the way, sit him down and say, "Okay, here we have a beautiful red stain on the new carpet. What are the rules about eating food in the family room?"

"We're not supposed to eat in the family room," the firstborn will acknowledge.

"Well, obviously you broke the rule."

"Yep, I guess I did."

"Then tell me, what should be your consequence?"

Let the firstborn come up with some solutions. Obviously, one solution is to turn him loose with a brush and plenty of carpet shampoo. But wait him out and see if he can come up with that idea himself. If he fails to show much imagination, tell him that you will probably have to have the carpet cleaned professionally and that you will take the cost of the cleaning out of his allowance at so much per week.

Disciplining the Second Born in a Two-Child Family

When disciplining children in the two-child family, remember that your second born can be a mix. He may have last born traits, but he could also have firstborn qualities, particularly if his older sibling is of a different sex. When you have one of each, you really have a firstborn girl and a firstborn boy on your hands.

Sometimes treating firstborns and second borns differently may result in one of the children claiming, "That's not fair—you gave her more than me!" Acknowledge that that might be true, but the next time the tables will be turned. This kind of "unfairness" evens out in the end.

Where you want to be scrupulously fair is in enforcing the rules. For example, be sure bedtimes are different for the two children—even if they're only a half hour apart. Be vigilant to send the second born to bed at 8:30, while the firstborn is allowed to stay up until 9:00. If either one gets to stay up later than the agreed-upon time, you will hear about it.

Make sure that responsibilities are different for the two children. Don't pile everything on the firstborn just because he proves himself to be reliable, conscientious, and willing to do it. Make a deliberate point to require the second born to hold up his or her end. Don't be afraid to give the second born the more menial task— raking the yard, dusting the bookshelves, or sweeping the garage—even though you know the firstborn would do a better job.

Bite your tongue if you feel like saying, "Why aren't

you like your brother [or sister]?" The last thing your children or your stepchildren need is comparisons. Believe me, they are making comparisons at a mile-a-minute rate anyway. When a parent or a stepparent comes along and starts comparing, it only makes the pain of comparison deeper, and discipline is all the harder to administer. Always remember the cardinal rule of Loving Discipline: Relationships come before rules. The reason for that is simple:

Rules without relationships lead to rebellion.[2]

Loving Discipline for Middles and Babies

Remember the middle child? He's the one who never made the photo album, the one who always feels squeezed, the one who's likely to go outside the home to find friends first, and the one who may be the best negotiator and mediator in the family. How do you discipline a middle child who isn't sticking to the rules or fulfilling responsibilities?

The best approach with most middle children is to ask them, "Why?" but not with the tone of voice that puts them in a corner. Instead, give them a chance to explain themselves while you listen and don't interrupt. You could say, "I'm interested in why—what was your thinking on this? I asked you to stay with your little sister, but you came home without her and let her walk home later by herself. That's not like you. What happened?"

Asking a middle child "Why?" in this fashion tells her that you want to hear her out. Also, ask the middle child to list the pluses and minuses of what happened. Ask her, "What have we learned from this situation?" All these things help make her mistake a teachable moment in her life.

As for those lovable babies of the family, be aware that when they goof up, they will try to get out of it. I know because I pulled it off for years (and sometimes I still try). The baby will look for somebody else to blame. If he claims, "It's Sister's fault," just smile and say, "Okay, Sister is in her room. You stay right here, I'm going to get her." Then bring big sister in and have her give her version of what happened.

The principle here is that when you feel your last born may be pulling your chain a little, try to go right to the source and find out what really happened. This inquiry may make you feel somewhat like Judge Wapner, a style that I'm usually not in favor of; but when dealing with the last born, remember that he's usually trying to get away with murder. You need to be firm as well as loving.

On the other side of the coin, your last born may be saying, "I'll show them!" If you think he's acted up because he feels discounted, overlooked, or put down, sit him down and ask him to tell you what is really going on. If his answer is sincere and not obviously manipulative, it can give you a better idea of what his discipline should be.

Remember, the baby is the slipperiest birth order of them all. When he breaks the rules, be sure you follow through with consequences. If you let him off the hook, he will shamelessly take advantage of everyone—and charm your socks off while he does it.

What Makes Loving Discipline So Difficult?

Now that I laid out my "perfect" system for disciplining children, you might be saying, "All this sounds great,

Dr. Leman. I guess you've been able to pull it off with your kids, but when I try some of this stuff with mine, they don't come back with just the right answers or just the right actions. It's still hard—very hard."

I couldn't agree more. I've had some hard moments myself while raising five kids (I still do, now and then). I still believe, however, that the Secrets of Loving Discipline are the best approach to raising responsible, accountable, and *affectionate* kids.

Before using Loving Discipline on your kids, however, be sure you have discipline in your own life. The best way to teach your kids to be responsible and accountable is to model those characteristics yourself.

Like anything that is worthwhile, Loving Discipline takes a little extra effort and often quite a bit more time. And it can be difficult on occasion because a certain "villain" lurks in the shadows, wanting to make you forget that relationships come before rules. This villain is an enemy who tries to turn your healthy authority into whaling the child verbally and even physically.

This enemy is easy to recognize but difficult to contain. We could call him Blended Family Enemy Number One, and we will take a closer look at how he operates in chapter 10.

NOTES

1. Kevin Leman, *Making Children Mind Without Losing Yours* (Old Tappan, NJ: Fleming H. Revell Co., 1984).

2. This statement is attributed to Josh McDowell, author and widely known speaker at high school and college campuses across the United States and other countries. Josh is also the father of four children.

"You Can't Tell Me What to Do—You're Not My Daddy!"

Disciplining the children may be the number one issue among most blended families, but anger is the villain that is causing most of the discipline problems.

You can almost bet that *everyone* in a blended family is mad at someone or someone is mad at them. Stepmoms are mad because they are treated like dirt or like the maid. Stepdads are mad because all they seem to be good for is paying the bills. Kids are mad because one of their parents is gone, sometimes forever. Children in the blended family are especially angry because they have been "ripped." They are hurt, and often they want to hurt back.

Be aware that the stepchild who is giving you a hard time is probably a discouraged child. Things didn't work out in his original family, and now it's gone. For a while he and his mom lived alone, and that was okay in some ways. But now his mother has remarried, and here come all these people he has never seen before. All of a sudden they are *here,* in his life and in his face.

Life is not working out at all. Discouragement covers him like a big wet blanket or a big black cloud. This kind of discouraged child may spend every day acting on the premise: "I've been kicked in the teeth by life, and now I'm going to kick back. I'm not doin' *one thing* that you want me to do."

What Causes the Anger?

Many of the issues facing the blended family are deep-seated causes of anger among its members, especially the kids. When we put these issues in the form of questions, we can see why the anger is there. Here are two familiar examples:

1. *"Why can't I see my dad more often? . . . Why can't Dad come back and live with us? . . . Why did Mommy have to die?"*

Questions like these pinpoint the *separation* and *loss* that the child feels after divorce or death. And now that he's in a new family, these feelings of loss affect his thoughts, decisions, and actions. Even if a child's family was dysfunctional (cold, neglectful, or abusive), it was still *his family* and he hated to lose it. His blended family reminds him daily of what he has lost. There is no instant cure for the pain caused by this separation and loss. Each person must learn to deal with it and let time be the healer.

2. *"Why did we have to move? . . . I liked it where we lived before . . . I miss my old friends."*

These comments voice the frustration a child feels from being *uprooted*. Moving into a blended family usually means tearing up roots and leaving the familiar surroundings that you knew earlier. The people in your blended family have lived in three homes in the past few years: the home that was broken up due to death or divorce; the home in which they lived with a single parent; the home in which they live now in a blended family.

Everyone in a blended family has to pass through these three phases, and even if their physical location stays the same throughout, the atmosphere of these homes is much different. No one in a blended family can feel a real sense of roots, at least not right away. It will take months, sometimes years, to get rid of the uprooted feeling.

Anger and Grief Go Hand in Hand

Working through anger caused by separation, loss, or uprootedness is a necessary part of working through the grief caused by the destruction of one of the most precious possessions in all the world—a person's original home and family. Grief includes at least three stages: shock, anger, and recovery.

Shock includes emotions like denial, numbness, and incredulity. When somebody in the shock stage says, "I can't believe it!" that's exactly what he means. He just simply can't accept what has happened. Shock can last a few minutes, or it can go on for several days or weeks. In extreme cases, it can last even longer.

For most of the people in a blended family, the shock wore off quite a while ago. But it's a good bet that most if not all, of them, are in stage number two—*anger,* which also includes fear, depression, and apprehensiveness.

Anger is the most dangerous stage of grief because a person can get stuck there for a long time. It's common for members of a blended family to bury their pain, but sooner or later it bubbles up when they have "had enough." I agree with Harold Bloomfield (author of *Making Peace in Your Stepfamily*) when he says:

> Buried pain eventually emerges as anger, depression, resentment, and guilt—destructive emotions that can tear a stepfamily apart. Repressed grief is one of the reasons why stepfamilies are so often troubled by angry outbursts and frequent bickering.[1]

Given time, anger fades and a person reaches the stage called *recovery*. She comes to terms with her pain, and, while it still may be there, she can accept what happened without feeling that same slow burn and bitterness that she knew in the past.

When everyone reaches at least some degree of recovery, you are not only a *blended* family, you are a *mended* family. Carolyn Johnson, a mother with four children who remarried a man with five, writes: "As we have mended our lives and those of our children, we have also mended our brokenness."[2]

Brokenness may not be the most politically or socially correct term these days, but in a blended family it is a fact that has to be dealt with. If you hope to guide your blended family toward mending its brokenness, you must first mend your own.

Realize, however, that mending the brokenness doesn't mean going back and assembling the broken pieces of what once was. There is no point in kidding yourself by entertaining the Humpty-Dumpty fantasy (besides, I have it on good authority from stepchildren and stepparents alike that Humpty Dumpty didn't fall, he was *pushed*). At any rate, Humpty Dumpty can't be put together again; you must build something *new,* and you do this by learning to accept the less-than-perfect situation.

Can You Live with Less Than Perfect?

It's amazing how many people have trouble accepting the less than perfect. Parents, stepparents, natural children, and stepchildren all want something they can't really have. They know they can't have it but they continue to tie themselves in knots by wanting it and expecting it; and when it doesn't happen, they continue to be angry.

To see how enmeshed you may be in a web of perfectionistic longing, see which of the following descriptions is most true of you. You can check more than one answer if you wish.

_____ *a. I'm having a hard time accepting the fact that we are different from a natural family, and being different bothers me.*

_____ *b. I fantasize a lot about how things used to be in my first family—especially the good times that we had. I want those good times back.*

_____ *c. I realize I can't go back and unscramble the eggs. I see my blended family as a new opportunity.*

_____ *d. We may be different from some other families, but every family has its problems. We can solve ours with commitment, hard work, patience, and plenty of love.*

Obviously, descriptions *c* and *d* are where you want to be. To get there, you may have to lower expectations that have been too high or too unrealistic. Blended families are different, but that doesn't make them inferior or second class. As your blended family mends its brokenness and learns to accept the less than perfect, a strange thing happens. You realize that what you had before wasn't really perfect either. In fact, *the perfect does not exist.*

All of us must find happiness and contentment in what we have. For blended families, the saying "Bloom where you are planted" is not just a prosaic platitude. It's a way of life.

Do not hurry anyone in your family who seems to be having a hard time getting over grief. Everyone grieves at his or her own pace. For some, grief comes like waves, for others, it settles in like a misty rain.

Some people wonder if it's healthy to go on grieving. After all, surely it's not good to dwell upon these things. Be positive with the person whose grief and anger continue. No one can do a person's grieving for him, and no one can set a time limit on how long someone else should grieve. It's more important to be patient and loving, realizing that a child's (or a spouse's) grief may be displayed in all kinds of symptoms: weeping, nightmares, bed wetting, depression, contempt, insolence, defiance, four-letter words, and angry outbursts of all kinds.

Guilt May Keep Fueling Your Anger

Another powerful force that is a deep-rooted cause of anger is guilt, which can be everywhere in a blended family. The new husband or wife, or both, feel guilty over previous failed marriages. Their children feel guilty, believing, "If only I had behaved better, Mommy and Daddy wouldn't have gotten divorced."

Without question, the birth orders most susceptible to guilt feelings in the blended family are the firstborns and only children—the perfectionists who "know" they could have or should have done more to keep the original family together.

Firstborns are notorious for their "musts" and their "shoulds." Their high expectations are constantly dogging their footsteps, and they usually see themselves as failing to do enough. Firstborns will spot the flaws every time and then magnify them into a federal case against themselves.

Firstborns do not handle change very well, and they don't like surprises. Unfortunately, a blended family goes through changes and surprises all the time, not all of them pleasant. On Monday, things can look pretty good, but by Wednesday or Thursday, somebody may be ready to call the cops—or the lawyer. And whenever there are conflicts and problems in the blended family, firstborns are the ones who are likely to think, *Surely, this must be my fault!*

Another birth order that is highly susceptible to guilty feelings is the middle child. What often does middle children in is their tremendous sense of loyalty and seeing themselves as mediators between warring parties. If there is a child in the family who might put himself squarely between Mom and Dad and wind up on the hook of guilty feelings, it could be the middle born.

As a rule, babies of the family are not guilt ridden people because they've been looking up to find others to blame ever since they can remember. This is not to say that a last born will never feel guilty, but typically last borns will give themselves the benefit of the doubt and try to fix the blame on others.

Mom Usually Feels Guiltiest of All

The bottom line is that the blended family is a breeding ground for guilt and a lot of people may be going around quietly saying, "If only I had done this . . ." or

"If only I had done that . . ." Probably the most susceptible of all is *Mom*. If her role is strictly that of natural mother (for example, she has remarried a man who has no children), then she will dwell on the guilt that comes when she sees the pain in the eyes of her children who still can't forgive her for leaving Dad.

And, of course, if Dad shows up every week or so for visitation or the children go to his house to visit, these guilt wounds keep getting reopened. Even a simple phone call from three states away can wipe away any progress that might have been made in recent weeks and months.

And when a woman winds up in the role of stepmother, she can face a double whammy. She will feel guilty about failing in the first marriage and leaving her children without a full-time father and, more often than not, in her blended family she soon learns that her stepchildren resent or reject her no matter how hard she tries to please them. She feels guilty again for failing in her role of stepmother, and her guilt may soon turn to anger when her stepchildren treat her with disrespect or let her know that their real mom is prettier, a better cook, or "nicer, because she lets me stay up when I go over there to visit."

Stepparents, in particular, are susceptible to guilty feelings. They are greatly relieved to hear that it's perfectly normal for a stepchild to reject a stepparent. And they are doubly relieved to hear that it's also normal if a stepparent doesn't love a stepchild with the same intensity he or she has for a natural child. As a caller on "Parent Talk" once told me, "You don't always fall in love with a man's children just because you fall in love with him."

I don't have an elaborate or surefire approach to dealing with guilty feelings. I do know it doesn't help to live in the past. There is no point in looking back. What is done is done. Look to the future, where the road will be hard, bumpy, and rough. Take smaller bites of life. Realize that you have made mistakes, but you can learn from them. *You can get through this.*

It is always healthy to own up to your mistakes. It takes two to tango, whether you're falling in love or out of it. But I am very concerned when I run onto someone who is obviously absorbing all of the guilt for what happened. Some blended family spouses (usually perfectionists or pleasers) are wallowing in guilt, which often expresses itself in anger toward other family members.

How to Deal with Guilt Attacks

To lessen guilty feelings, it helps to own up to the fact that life isn't perfect, marriages aren't perfect, and *you* are not perfect. The guilt you may be carrying can be the impetus for bad decisions about your blended family. The best way to guard against this is to bounce all major decisions off your spouse, who is in a much better position to be objective about the situation.

So, when you have a guilt attack, share it with your mate who can remind you, "Honey, listen, you are beating yourself up unnecessarily." I'm not suggesting you go to your mate strictly to get off the hook. But trust your mate to give you reaffirmation or to help you correct yourself if you have gotten off course.

For many people, particularly firstborns, guilty feelings do not let go easily. As Erma Bombeck said, "Guilt is a gift that keeps on giving" (and giving, and giving). But don't let guilt turn into anger. Admit your failures (yes, even if you're a perfectionist), but don't wallow in them.

If your faith includes a personal relationship with God, this is the opportunity to put your faith to the test. My own faith tells me that we humans tend to look at life *vertically,* seeing certain people or groups as higher or lower than others, according to how they have performed. I believe, however, that God sees us from a *horizontal* point of view. Everyone is on the same level. The person in her first marriage is not inherently better than someone in her second or third. The Maker and Giver of life loves us all the same.

Among the viewers of the *realFAMILIES.com* television program was a woman with two daughters, ages eleven and nine, who married a man with a son, thirteen, and a daughter, ten. Besides all of the obvious birth order collisions between all the firstborns in their blended family, she and her husband had to put up with an insane ruling by a judge who decided that her husband's children would live with their natural mother every other week throughout the year.

Hampered by being unable to establish any real relationship with her stepchildren on an "every other week" basis, the stepmother was the constant target of their angry and often snide remarks. Lately, they had been coming back from the week at their mother's house to tell her and her husband (their dad) that their mother would soon be getting remarried and they would be moving to a beautiful new home that would include a pool, a volleyball court, and a personal TV and VCR for each of them in their own rooms.

"My stepchildren are constantly boasting about all the things they are going to have when they live with their mother on a permanent basis, which they plan to do just as soon as possible," our caller said. She realized it was childish, but she had to admit that she was feeling upset with her stepchildren and their continuous emphasis on material things. Her husband was also upset, feeling he wasn't a good provider because he couldn't buy the family a new home, TV's, and all those other goodies.

"When my husband started talking that way, I felt guilty because I thought I might have been coming across as if I were not thankful for what we did have," she confessed. "Then I was angry with the children, who were acting immature, but I was being as immature as they were and that made me feel even more guilty. I've ended up feeling that I'm not much of a Christian."

My on-the-air advice was, "Don't do that to yourself. There are enough people in life who will dump on you without adding to it from within. The wonderful thing about being a Christian is understanding thoroughly what the word *grace* means. If you ever need a little encouragement on God's grace, look at King David. I mean, this guy was really not a very nice guy. He committed adultery with Bathsheba and then set up her husband to be killed in battle.[3] Still, he ended up God's favorite. If God can forgive and love David, he can forgive and love you and me.[4] I find joy in that myself."

I hope you find joy in that thought, too. If anyone needs huge doses of God's grace daily, it is the stepparent in a blended family. The stepparent constantly runs into those who aren't accepting, who are bitter, angry, and even vindictive. As the stepparent, you will sometimes make mistakes. You can lose it, blow your top, say things you don't really mean (or perhaps you really *do* mean them!). Remember, that no matter what, God always loves and accepts you.

What About My Child's Guilt over the Divorce?

As for dealing with a child who is loaded with guilty feelings about your divorce, one of your best strategies is to be vulnerable to that child. Let your child know that you feel guilty about the divorce, but you also know that you could not have gone on with the situation as it was. Then reassure your child that he or she did not cause the divorce.

As one mother told me, "I've spent a lot of time with my daughter explaining to her that I'm the guilty one, not her. I have a lot of baggage, especially the guilt about not having the kids with me during all those years of separation when I could only see them a total of about three months a year. Then I also have guilt because I'm the one who broke off the marriage with their dad."

This mom knows that it takes more than one talk to absolve a child's feeling of guilt. In fact, it is typical to hear a child say, "I know Mom keeps telling us kids it's really not our fault, but I don't think I really believe her."

Patiently and lovingly, keep reassuring your child that it wasn't his or her fault. One way to approach the problem is to say, "Honey, I know that anything Daddy and I do affects you, but the choice was not a choice that *you made me make*. I made that choice myself and so did Daddy. I know it's normal to feel guilty, but you have no real reason because you had nothing to do with it."

Ex Marks an Angry Spot

In many blended family situations, the actions of the ex-spouse can make everyone angry. Here is a real-life scenario:

When Dawn got remarried, she brought her two sons, Reese and Tony, to the blended family while her new husband, Jerry, brought his two daughters, Shannon and Megan. Dawn's ex-husband, Walter, gave them no problems. He continued to treat Dawn and his boys as he had treated them before the divorce—with little or no interest.

Jerry's ex-wife, Raquel, was a different story. She was full of rage over Jerry's remarriage, and because she had custody of Shannon and Megan, any visits they made to see their dad were always tense affairs. Raquel obviously begrudged any time her daughters spent in Jerry's home, particularly under the influence of their stepmother, Dawn, who became fond of the girls and wanted to be more a part of their lives. But when Dawn asked to attend parent/teacher conferences at the school, Raquel would simply not hear of it.

Raquel continually sniped about what clothes the children could wear while visiting their dad. Even a hairstyle Dawn created for Shannon became a major issue. Raquel threw out presents and candies sent home with the children after holidays, and she told the children that they weren't allowed to keep anything from their father's home.

"The worst part is that the kids were brought into all of this," Dawn said. "They came back and told us what Raquel wanted us to know. She sent messages through them."

That Raquel used her children to send messages back to her ex-husband and his new wife was not rare or unusual. Divorced parents often play "war games"[5] and put their children right in the middle of the battle. When Raquel sent messages back to her ex-husband and his new wife by way of her children, she was playing what I call *carrier pigeon*. Another favorite game is *stool pigeon*, in which parents ask the children to be spies. The children are to report back to their blended home about what is going on in the visitation home; or when they go to the visitation home, they are pumped about what is going on in their blended family home.

Stirring up trouble is another back-and-forth blended family game. The ex-spouse fills the children full of hateful thoughts about the other ex-spouse, and then sends them over for their regular visit, which will probably not turn out well because the children have been brainwashed to be angry upon their arrival. Or, when the children come for a visit, the ex-spouse pumps them full of negative remarks, and sends them back home to the custodial parent full of anger, confusion, and doubt.

Never Trash Your Ex to Your Child

Stirring up trouble was a favorite game played by Wanda's ex-husband, Dennis, who would fill his eleven-year-old daughter, Paige, full of reasons that her mother was the one who had caused the divorce and "destroyed" their family.

"I had Paige in counseling for a while last year because she was still full of so much anger about the way her father left," Wanda related. "Dennis had several affairs, and when he finally decided to leave me for good, he told the kids before he even told me, so they have had that burden to carry. Our son, Toby, was five at the time and couldn't quite understand, but Paige, who was nine, was terribly hurt. She keeps saying, 'I've got to know the truth, I want to know exactly why my dad left.'"

"Does Paige ever see her dad, and does she ask him?" I wondered.

"Oh, she sees him all right—he has visitation rights every other weekend. But every time she talks to Dennis about it, he takes no responsibility whatever. He just rehashes all the trouble we had before he left. And, of course, he never tells her about the affairs. Instead of trying to help her understand, he just feeds her anger, and she comes back home blaming me."

"You've got to remember several things," I pointed out. "First, Paige is a firstborn. Naturally, she wants to know all the details. But the details in this case are that Dad had repeated affairs, and she's really too young to know about that."

"That's what I thought," Wanda responded. "I may tell her someday when she's older, but she doesn't need that right now."

I pointed out to Wanda that she was being very wise by not "trashing" her husband to her child. Wanda had every right to feel the inclination to strike back and tell her daughter what a no-good louse Dennis was, but she wasn't letting her feelings dictate her actions. She was thinking it through and taking the wise course. What she needed, however, were some ideas on how to handle her daughter's simmering anger.

Learning How to Regulate Your Emotional Balloon

In blended families, almost everyone may be carrying simmering anger of one kind or another because of what has happened. Add collisions of birth order and the crisscrossing of the life-styles and life themes of the parents and the children, and simmering anger can erupt at any moment.

To picture simmering anger for my clients, I use two analogies: a volcano and an inflated balloon. Volcanos bubble and sputter, occasionally spout smoke and ashes, and sometimes flow intermittently. And when a volcano really blows, it can destroy just about everything. Mount St. Helens proved that.

But while all you can do is wait for volcanos to finally blow, balloons are another story. The members of a blended family all have emotional balloons inside. Every day strife, tension, and stress all put in a little more air. Unless something is done, a person's balloon can stretch so tight that one more puff of air and—BOOM!

Unlike the volcano, however, the balloon can be regulated. You may remember being a kid and having a balloon all blown up to just about capacity. Then you'd take hold of the neck of the balloon, stretch it out and let out just a little bit of air at a time. This would make a terrible noise—a screech that would drive your mother crazy. While the noise was unpleasant, the net result was that the balloon went down a little and the probability that it would pop was greatly reduced.

It is the same with members of your blended family. As they get things that are hard to talk about out on the table, there may be some discomfort; there may be a little noise that is hard to listen to, but it's a lot better than BOOM!

How to Handle Your Mini Mount St. Helens

My advice to Wanda or any parent who has to handle anger that is going off in her face includes the following:

1. *Expect the best from everyone, but don't be surprised when anger does erupt.* Like the molten rock in a volcano, anger is bubbling and seething beneath the surface, and every now and then there is bound to be an explosion. It will not help much, however, if you explode back.

2. *Try to identify the real problem.* It may be the other person's problem completely, and realizing that will keep you from getting sucked into trading angry shots with the other person.

3. *To get at the real reason behind your stepchild's anger, listen for his or her feelings.* I touched on this briefly in chapter 7 when talking about how to deal with your spouse, but active listening is also a valuable tool to use with children. To actively listen means that you are trying to reflect back the feelings you are hearing your stepchild express, but as you do so you never judge, advise, lecture, or play travel agent for guilt trips.

When you actively listen, you are trying to show the child *empathy*—putting yourself in his or her shoes. As you actively listen, don't analyze or ask a lot of questions. When reflecting a child's feelings, one of the best phrases to use is, "Sounds like" as in, "Sounds like you are very upset with me [or your brother, or your stepdad]."

Note that there is a difference between active listening and parroting. For example, if your stepchild says, "Oh, what's the use, nobody ever listens to me," you will be guilty of parroting if you say, "So you think, 'What's the use, nobody ever listens.'" If you want to reflect your child's feelings, however, say something like, "Sounds like you're discouraged because we don't seem to hear what you're saying—tell us more."

That phrase "tell us [or tell me] more" is a very handy tool. Use it often to get the child to tell you what is on her mind. And bite your tongue when a brilliant flash of genius inspires you to lecture or give advice. If 90 percent of the lectures and pieces of "good advice" from parents were laid end to end, it would probably be a good thing. I'm not saying you should never give your child advice; I am saying, try to wait for your child to ask you for it. If you feel you must offer advice, particularly to an angry child, always preface it with, "I could be wrong but . . ."

Another effective technique that I have used for many years when dealing with an angry child during a counseling session is that when you see the child ready to tear up, just reach across and gently touch him—on the arm or on the shoulder. You don't have to say much, just let your look of compassion tell him that you want to be supportive as you listen to the feelings he's expressing.

Wanda sat down with Paige and tried the steps I discussed above. She was pleasantly surprised at the results. Like every firstborn, Paige had taken the full brunt of what was going wrong in the family. As it turned out, she was a typical firstborn girl who felt very much in the middle of her mom and dad. She wanted to give both of them equal time and equal love. A pleaser, Paige didn't want either one of them angry with her. And due to that special connection that is always there between daddy and daughter, she had somehow felt guilty about his leaving. She needed reassurance it wasn't her fault, and she told her mother she was sorry she had been so angry with her.

Don't Be a Septic Tank

Like anything else, active listening is not some kind of magical tool that will instantly dissipate every stepchild's anger. When a child continues to be angry, you want to try to listen, but under no circumstances settle for being a septic tank. It will do no good to constantly take garbage—and worse—from the members of your blended family.

Let the snippy eight-year-old or the obscenity-spouting teenager know theirs is unacceptable behavior. Be firm in saying, "I cannot and will not accept this kind of talk." At the same time, don't deny your stepchild's feelings. Let her know that she probably has a right to feel angry, but emphasize that she has to work out a more acceptable way to express her anger.

My best advice to the parents of a blended family is to understand that anger is a given, not necessarily an evil. Anger is not something to wring your hands over or stuff deep inside and deny. Anger isn't something to be lectured or preached about. Anger needs to be processed, diluted, and worked through. I believe that it's possible to be good *and* angry. It is not a sin to be angry, but expressing and dealing with anger in positive ways is the real challenge.

Remember the balloon analogy, how letting a little air out can make all the difference? One way to help everybody "let a little air out" is by having family meetings that include "I'm angry about . . ." sessions. Gather everyone in a circle and lay down some ground rules. First, be sure everyone understands the difference between an "I" message and a "you" message.

Briefly, a "you" message is stated as an accusation or an attack, as in, "You bug me . . . You are a slob . . . You don't care what happens . . ."

An "I" message is sent in an effort to be transparent and let the other person know how you feel or even to admit vulnerability or weakness. You might say, "I get really frustrated when the chores aren't done . . . I hate being told to go to bed early . . . I wish our family didn't fight so much . . ."

Consistently using "I" messages is difficult, and there will be times when you will send "you" messages, but at least you can get people thinking about the difference between hurling verbal harpoons at one another and trying to air feelings to find some solutions.

In an "I'm angry about . . ." session, there is to be no putting people down or interrupting. Everyone can be invited to start out with, "I've got something to say. I'm angry or upset or irritated about [whatever is bothering that person]." Let everyone know that you are all there to talk about what is making you angry. Everyone should be trying to find out what he or she can do to solve little problems before there is an explosion.

If you can keep this kind of meeting under control and inject some humor at certain points, it will go a long way toward encouraging direct communication among family members. It will also make everyone sensitive to who is angry and what they are angry about.

One blended family mom told me that her insistence on family meetings to get feelings out in the open had really paid off. Her first challenge was getting the family to sit down together long enough to even have a meeting! "The stepchildren who came into our home had a hard time with family meetings at first because they'd been able to eat when they wanted and then just take off," she explained. "But I insisted that they stay and that we all share our day together and any feelings that we might have building up. For us, family meetings have been invaluable."

Anger Caused Tammy's Magnificent Obsession

When Ginger, a firstborn girl, married Scott, a last born, three years ago, she thought that she and her son, Jimmy, who was five at the time, would have fewer problems blending with her new husband because his two children were in the custody of their mother. Less than two years later, however, that situation changed. Wanting more freedom to "explore her potential," Scott's ex-wife, Vanessa, asked him to take full custody of Tammy, ten, and Billy, eight.

Scott agreed, and the new arrangement brought out ambivalent feelings in Tammy, Scott's firstborn daughter, who had always experienced continual tension with her mother, an only child who really didn't understand children or want to be a parent. Tammy had lived for the weekends and summers when she could visit Daddy, and she felt a very special link to him. At the same time, she hated the idea of her father being married to another woman, especially Ginger, with whom she hadn't hit it off right from the start.

Tammy's younger brother, Billy, wasn't ambivalent at all—he was just depressed. Hurt by his mother's decision to give him up, Billy went into an emotional shell when he moved into Scott and Ginger's home. No matter what Ginger tried to do, eight-year-old Billy would not come out of that shell except to fight with Jimmy, who at age seven, now presented a real threat to Billy's previously unchallenged position as baby of the family.

Naturally, Jimmy wasn't too happy either. As an only child, he had ruled the roost and was the "little man" of the family ever since his dad had left his mother five years earlier. Now a grownup had moved in on his man-of-the-family turf, and a stepbrother was trying to get more attention than he did.

A diagram of their family shows how the different birth orders were squaring off at the time Ginger came to see me:

Ginger (firstborn pleaser)	Scott (last born attention-getter)
Jimmy—7	Tammy—10
	Billy—8

As soon as Tammy and Billy moved in, the problems started. Billy and Jimmy squared off to fight over being baby prince of the family, but their squabbles were nothing compared to the message Ginger got from her stepdaughter: "She set out to monopolize her dad and punish me in every way she could," Ginger related on her first visit to my office.

"And I take it she has succeeded?"

"She's succeeding all right," Ginger said bitterly. "She's been very snippy with me from the start, very strong-willed, and she just tries to make my life miserable any way she can. They are simple things, like disrupting whatever I say or making disparaging remarks about the meals I cook, but she saves her best tricks for trying to get between her dad and me."

"Her best tricks? For instance?"

"Any time she can possibly get Scott to spend time with her rather than with me, she'll do it. She overheard us planning a weekend away together, and the next day she came home and told her dad that she had been picked as starting pitcher for her softball team in a big game that weekend. She was counting on him to come watch her play. What really burned me was that Scott gave in and didn't even say anything to me about trying to go on our weekend another time. It's as if he can't see what Tammy is doing."

I pointed out to Ginger that, first of all, she had two firstborn collisions going, one between herself and her stepdaughter, and the other between Tammy and Ginger's son, Jimmy. Even though they were three years apart, they were both firstborns, and because Jimmy was a super firstborn (an only child), he had mannerisms that really irritated his stepsister. When Tammy's brother, Billy, got in arguments or fights with Jimmy, Tammy loved to back Billy up and blame Jimmy for whatever happened. Naturally, her dad tended to believe her because she was older.

As for Billy and Jimmy, here we had a baby of the family bumping smack up against an only child, who had always had everything his own way. An only child can easily have characteristics of a firstborn, but he can also be a baby in many ways because he's always had all the attention.

As for Billy going into his "shell," this behavior was a ploy to get Ginger's attention, and when he didn't think he was succeeding, he would get into fights with Jimmy—a sure-fire way to get the attention he wanted.

Ginger Was Part of a Triangle

A typical setting for anger in the blended family is in the various triangles that are constantly forming. Loyalty is usually the issue in a family triangle, which forms when two family members have some kind of conflict (are angry with each other) and they both pressure a third member of the family for support, relief, or sympathy. This can cause a wrangle that makes all three people angry, and more than likely, others in the family also join the party.

I explained to Ginger that she was definitely part of a triangle consisting of herself, her husband, and her stepdaughter, Tammy. She and Tammy were the ones in conflict, and they were both looking to Scott for support and sympathy.

"A minute ago you said something very profound," I told Ginger. "You observed that it's as if Scott can't see what Tammy is doing. Do you remember the old song, 'Smoke Gets In Your Eyes'? Well, in this case, guilt over his divorce is the smoke in Scott's eyes, and—it's true—he doesn't see what his daughter is doing."

"Then what can I do?" Ginger wanted to know.

"Your first task is to remove yourself from this triangle that has formed among you, Tammy, and Scott. The best approach is to make Scott aware of what's happening. Sit down with him and explain what Tammy is trying to do, but don't be bitter about it. Tell him that you want to become a real mom to Tammy but you're going to need his help."

Ginger did as I suggested, and at first Scott just couldn't believe what she was telling him. But when he started being more aware of Tammy's ploys, it wasn't long until he told his wife, "I think I see what you're talking about."

Together they worked on "weaning" Tammy away from her dad. Ginger still gave Scott plenty of space to take lots of father/daughter time, but she also started moving in to spend time with Tammy as well. When Tammy saw that her stepmother wasn't trying to take her dad away, she relented and began sharing openly with Ginger how she felt. Eventually, Ginger and Tammy became good friends, and Ginger knew she had made a real breakthrough when Tammy started calling her "Mom."

Tammy's little brother, Billy, was a tougher nut to crack. His problem was that he needed attention from his dad, who had been tending to pay more attention to Tammy because of her fights with his wife. I pointed out to Scott that when you spend 90 percent of your time on one child in the family, it's a good bet you're neglecting everybody else. When Scott took my advice and started giving Billy more attention, his little shell began to crack.

And Ginger and Scott didn't forget her son, Jimmy, either. At my urging, they took him on special outings with just the two of them. As he basked in their undivided attention, they learned that he made charming company for adults, which is typical of an only child. They both realized that having an older brother and sister move in didn't really change Jimmy's natural birth order. He was still an only child and needed to be treated that way.

Turn Frustration to Forgiveness

Living in a stepfamily requires skill in handling two kinds of anger—theirs *and* yours. It's all very well to encourage family members to express feelings as you actively listen to an irate stepchild or spouse going off in your face, but just how do you deal with the rising frustration that is filling your own emotional balloon to the bursting point? Here is a simple plan for keeping your cool when frustration strikes.

Frustration is stage one in moving toward an angry outburst. Simply stated, it means *not getting what you want.* If you are frustrated long enough, you are likely to begin to lose patience. Now you are moving into stage two— *indignation* (what some call "getting a little bit irritated"). You begin to think about how awful this frustrating problem is becoming. You start to tell yourself, "This isn't right . . . I don't deserve this . . . I will demand my rights!"

As David Augsburger puts it, "Anger is a demand. It may be a demand that you hear me, or that you recognize my worth. Or that you see me as precious and worthy to be loved. Or that you respect me. Or, 'Let go of my arm.' Or, 'Quit trying to take control of my life.'"[6]

At this point you are entering stage three—*heated anger,* which, temporarily at least, can turn reason into insanity and love into hatred. Your emotional balloon can take no more, and you explode—snapping at your spouse or your kids, cuffing somebody on the ear, maybe even whaling somebody with a belt.

When living in a stepfamily starts to make you feel stepped on, you can head off explosive anger by using cognitive discipline. Don't follow your feelings; think it through by asking yourself: "Is this frustration a catastrophe or just an annoyance? If it is really an annoyance, must I think it is 'awful'?" Then ask yourself: "Okay, I admit I'm getting irritated, but is this the end of the world? Does this *really* matter? A hundred years from now, will it make *any* difference? In fact, in *one year,* or even *one week,* will I even remember this?"

At this point, you may be thinking, *All Leman is doing is giving me a fancy way to count to ten.* Maybe so, but the more you are able to cut frustration off at the ankles and not let it turn into anger, the more you will be able to cope with the times that are truly explosive. In other words, there are many situations where you can fight back by simply choosing not to fight back at all. You don't have to like what is going on, but you can accept it and hope and pray for better days ahead, which eventually do come.

And to deal a death blow to frustration or anger, you can always whip out your most powerful weapon of all—*forgiveness.* I'm not going to preach a sermon on forgiving, but it is sort of interesting that the Bible has a great deal to say on the subject. One of my favorite passages instructs me to forgive "seventy times seven."[7] That's 490 times. When Sande leaves me to watch our "late in life blessings," Hannah and Lauren, I like to say, tongue in cheek, that after I've forgiven some strong wills, a few spills, and some other thrills, I still have about 479 "forgives" to go!

That's really not how it works, of course. I heard our pastor say once that seventy times seven is not to be taken literally. Good thing. Otherwise, a lot of parents and stepparents wouldn't take long to run out of forgiveness. On some days a lot of stepmoms would be fresh out by noon!

Actually, I'm told that forgiving seventy times seven really means forgiving *indefinitely,* on an *unlimited* basis. Your blended family is a perfect laboratory to experiment with this radical idea. Actually, it's more than just an experiment. Forgiveness is to the blended family what oil is to an engine. Forgiveness is the Armor All that keeps a blended family from cracking and splitting under its own heat.

Forgiveness is love in action; in fact, "Forgiveness is love's toughest work and love's biggest risk."[8] So, why not take the risk? It beats feeling stepped on every time!

NOTES

1. Harold H. Bloomfield with Robert B. Kory, *Making Peace in Your Stepfamily* (New York: Hyperion, 1993), 26.

2. Carolyn Johnson, *How to Blend a Family* (Grand Rapids: Pyranee Books, Zondervan Publishing House, 1989), 9.

3. See 2 Samuel, Chapter 11.

4. See Psalm 51.

5. Bloomfield, *Making Peace in Your Stepfamily,* 251.

6. David Augsburger, *Caring Enough to Confront* (Ventura: Regal

Books, © 1973 under the title *The Love Fight* by Harold Press, Scottsdale, PA), 38.

7. See Matthew 18:21–22.

8. Lewis B. Smedes, *Forgive and Forget* (New York: Pocket Books, 1984), 12.

From the Win/Lose Blender to Win/Win Blending

As this book winds down, I have only one more question:

As you and your mate go about blending your family, is your approach win/lose or win/win?

There really isn't much in between. As you deal with your kids, at the bottom line, your leadership style is one or the other:

- Win/Lose—"I win, you lose. I maintain my position as the boss, the controller, the one who dominates this situation. Nuts to relationships. My rules are all that count."

- Win/Win—"We both win. As the parent I have done my best to be in healthy authority. I've listened to you, empathized with you, and then tried to do the best thing for our family. The whole is always more important than the parts."

To achieve win/win blending, it will take patience, a lot of hard work, and *organized persistence*. I believe it helps to look at a blended family as a corporation of sorts, of which you and your spouse are co-CEOs. To help yourselves hang in there in the face of the relentless stress and pressure, I suggest putting the following paragraph up on your bulletin board, or refrigerator door, and reading it often. These words are attributed to Ray Kroc, founder of McDonald's world-encompassing hamburger chain, which has sold umpteen billion Big Macs and such and shows no signs of stopping:

> Press on: Nothing in the world can take the place of persistence. Talent will not; nothing is more common than unsuccessful individuals with talent. Genius will not; unrewarded genius is almost a proverb. Education will not; the world is full of educated derelicts. Persistence and determination alone are omnipotent.[1]

Now I realize Mr. Kroc's words could sound a little flowery to someone up to his or her hips in stepfamily alligators, but keep studying them until they sink in. When that happens, you'll be able to move beyond simply trying to avoid being stepped on or stepping on others in your blended family, and you can concentrate on your real goal: putting together a home where everyone feels respected, accepted, and loved. Idealistic? Sure, but it can and does happen, even though you may start out thinking you won't make it through the first year. As one stepmom told me, "I thought he was too hard on *my* children. He thought I was too strict with *his* children. Everyone was angry with everyone else. When my husband and I were going to have our first child together, his children thought they were going to be pushed aside. All this and more went on during our first year of trying to blend, and I kept saying, 'If we survive this year with God's help, we can survive anything.' And you know, we did. It's been amazing."

Sure, there will be days when you will want to chuck it all. "They" won and you lost and you don't need this anymore. But if you *persevere*, you can climb Blended Family Mountain and get to the summit called Win/ Win.

In this book I've shared the stories of people I've counseled or interviewed, and you've seen how many of them are "hanging in there," sometimes on a three-inches-forward, two-inches-back basis, but they're making progress and that's what counts.

In this chapter, I want you to meet two outstanding examples of how the win/win approach works in a blended family. I suppose you could call them "success stories." I like to see them as ordinary people from real life who have had their blended family problems, but they solved them anyway with faith, creative ingenuity, and that little quality Ray Kroc calls *persistence*.

Best Blended Family of Them All?

I believe that whenever a blended family is hitting on all birth order cylinders, it's because they share the same positive, healthy, wholesome values and beliefs. They have a system for operating their family that includes rules and order tempered by love, compassion—and plenty of good humor. That was true in the home of

Diane, a firstborn pleaser, and Alex, an easygoing middle child.

Part of what makes them an outstanding success story is the way they handled their problems during that notorious first eighteen months that so many blended families talk about. How they got over the hump and continued to blend so well has to be inspirational and helpful to anyone who has ever taken the plunge into the sea of stepfamily living. Today Diane and Alex have four children in all, and their blended family diagram stacks up like this:

Diane (firstborn
pleaser)
    Colleen—11
    Colin—7

Alex (easygoing middle
child)
    Samantha—12

Born to Diane and Alex
Sara—2

As part of the research for this book, I asked for volunteers at my seminars who were in blended families and willing to share their experiences. Diane and Alex had given me their names, and when I interviewed them, I learned that they had just celebrated their fourth anniversary. Their marriage and blended family was obviously on solid ground for several reasons, including:

She was a widow and he a widower, her mate dying of cancer and his in an auto accident. While losing their spouses was traumatic, their first marriages had closure, and they were able to approach the building of a new family without having to deal with ex-spouses and all of the problems those relationships so often entail.

Their other advantage was the "perfect" match of their

own life-styles and life themes. A compliant firstborn, Diane was a pleaser who, when asked what the greatest challenge in blending her family had been, said: "Learning how to keep everybody happy." Diane had loving parents, especially her dad who had always been there for her. She had typical firstborn traits—conscientious, organized, and even a touch perfectionistic—but her life theme rang loud and clear: "I only count when I keep everything going smoothly and everyone is happy."

Diane was what I call a positive pleaser. She liked who she was, and she also liked nurturing and care-giving. She had achieved an excellent balance between pleasing people, especially her blended family members, and having them treat her with respect in return.[2]

Alex, born third in a family of four that included two older sisters as well as a younger brother, was the epitome of the easygoing middle child: sociable and outgoing but still laid-back, a skilled negotiator and mediator. In addition, while growing up with two older sisters, he had learned a lot about what women like and don't like, how they feel about things, and how they want to be treated.

A highly successful middle manager in a dry goods manufacturing firm, Alex was well-known for his win/win approach to people. His life theme was: "I only count when everybody wins," and he carried that theme right into his remarriage to Diane.

"Nobody Can Ever Replace My Mom!"

As well matched as Alex and Diane were, the first eighteen months of their marriage was no picnic. Diane recalled that at several points she became "just a little bit discouraged—maybe a *lot* discouraged. I wasn't sure we would make it."

One of their major problems was not having ex-spouses in the picture. They both had daughters who had grieved a great deal over their dead parents. In fact, when Diane and Alex got married, Samantha was still grieving heavily, which was part of why the first eighteen months were so difficult. As Harold Bloomfield points out, "After the death of a parent, the children . . . idealize the memory of the dead parent. When a widow(er) re-marries, the loyalty issues for children can be even more difficult than after a divorce."[3]

Diane had waited almost two and a half years to re-marry, and she had spent a lot of time helping her daugh-ter, Colleen, get through her grief concerning her dad. Colin, who was not yet two when his daddy died, ad-justed more quickly. Alex had lost his wife about eigh-teen months before remarrying, and his daughter, Samantha, was still taking her mother's death hard.

I was impressed to learn that they both followed a rule that I highly recommend for all single parents: When they had begun dating, they kept their dating relation-ship completely separate from their children in its initial stages. They would meet somewhere for a date, and neither one of them came to the other's home until their relationship had progressed to where they thought it might get serious.

When they married, they included all three children in the wedding. Colleen and Colin had no trouble accepting Alex as their new dad, but Alex's daughter, Samantha, was slow to accept Diane. She missed her natural mother very much, and during the first year of the new blended family's existence, Samantha would often tell Diane ve-hemently, "Nobody can *ever* replace my mom!"

Diane understood how Samantha felt because her own daughter, Colleen, had gone through the same thing. In fact, Colleen still had down days as she fondly remembered her father. Whenever Samantha would get depressed or angry, Diane wisely sat down with her and asked, "Tell me about your mom. I'd like to know more about her."

During those first months, Samantha would say little, but eventually she did begin to open up. It helped that her stepmother wasn't defensive and didn't put her down for continuing to feel sad about her real mom.

Fortunately, Diane and Alex had gotten counseling after losing their mates and were aware that their daughters had to grieve at their own individual pace. They also understood that their grief would generate anger that would only increase the likelihood of a major birth order collision.

Only Child Meets Bossy Firstborn

When the family blended, Samantha was eight, Colleen was seven, and Colin was three. An assertive firstborn who liked to mother her little brother and even give him time-outs when she thought he had been naughty, Colleen's life theme was a familiar version of, "I only count when I'm calling the shots."

Unfortunately, Colleen's stepsister, Samantha, also felt that way—in spades. As an only child, she had never enjoyed bossing a little brother around, but she could go Colleen one better: She had always been the center of attention, never having to share the spotlight with anyone, and she had been the apple of her daddy's eye, particularly after her mother's tragic death in a six-car freeway pileup.

Samantha's life theme was the classic viewpoint of the only child who has always been "the special jewel": "I only count when I get my way." Of course, Colleen, only a year younger, wasn't at all interested in giving Samantha her way, and when the girls had to share a room they butted heads—big time.

Colleen's little brother, Colin, just stood back and watched his sister and stepsister go at it. Many times he couldn't quite see what the fuss was about because Colin was the exact opposite of his uptight perfectionistic older sister. Disorganized and rather helpless at times, Colin was the classic clown who would often diffuse potentially tense situations by getting everybody laughing. His life theme was, "I only count when I make people laugh."

While Colleen and Samantha were both perfectionists, there were some differences: Samantha was analytical while Colleen was very creative. Samantha brought home the best grades in math while Colleen got top grades in English, especially creative writing and social studies.

At first Diane had despaired of ever seeing Colleen and Samantha get along and live in peace. One of Samantha's biggest problems was that as an only child she had never had to share *anything*. During the first months of being in a new family, Samantha labeled everything that was hers— every toy, every book, you name it. She even asked Diane to sew name tags in her clothes so Colleen wouldn't steal them. If Colleen or Colin went out to the kitchen for a snack after school, Samantha was right there to let them know that all the Twinkies or cookies—whatever—had been purchased for her lunch and no one else's.

Two Controllers Kept Careful Score

Jealousy was a big problem, which was caused, of course, by the controlling life-styles of both girls. Skilled scorekeepers, they kept careful track of what was done for one that wasn't done for the other. For example, if Samantha got a new sweater, Colleen was sure to want one as well—and certainly it had to cost the same amount of money. If Diane or Alex helped Colleen with her homework, Samantha wanted equal time.

As Diane put it, "They both wanted to control the home as far as who was the oldest and who did this and who did that, and when they got angry with each other, it was natural for Alex and me both to automatically side with our natural children. He was saying, 'Why are your kids such brats?' and I was saying, 'Why is your kid so impossible?' We often wound up pretty miffed with one another."

I commented to Diane that she and her husband had been drawn into one of those favorite blended family games called *playing favorites*. Fortunately, both of them had realized that was what was happening. They put their heads together, and instead of letting the kids get them into more arguments, they worked out several practical plans for guiding the two girls into a much better relationship.

To help them learn to share, they worked out schedules and lists, and insisted everyone, Colin included, sign up for his or her turn. They also had sign-up lists for choosing chores.

To nip jealousy in the bud, Diane and Alex worked hard on learning each child's strengths and weaknesses and scheduled one-on-one time with each child. And they made sure that each child got help on homework when it was needed.

During the first year, especially, when anyone needed disciplining, the natural parent did it, whether it was a rare spanking, or some other form of reasonable consequences. By the end of the second year, both Alex and

Diane were able to discipline their stepchildren as well as their natural children without feeling tension.

Everyone Was Ready for Sara's Arrival

A positive addition to the family had been Sara, born to Diane and Alex about two and a half years after their marriage. While pregnant with Sara, Diane had run across several articles on avoiding displacement when a new child arrives. She got involved in a prenatal program at a local hospital that included a "Big Brother/Big Sister" class. They all attended as a family, and the three children got big brother and big sister T-shirts. They also got to see the delivery room where the new baby would come into the world.

Diane and Alex took special pains with Colin, who was only four when Sara was born. Before Sara arrived, Diane talked to Colin, saying, "The new baby won't be able to walk like you can or talk like you can. And think of this: the new baby is going to have to take *ten* naps a day and you only have to take *one*." She also talked to Colin about putting his special toys up high on a shelf so that when the baby came, the toys would be "safe."

"Colleen and Samantha were a little older, of course, and they seemed very positive and excited about my having Sara," Diane recalled, "but still we thought it would be fun to give each of them a gift from their new little sister on the day she was born. They each got a Sony Walkman with the same note: 'When I cry or when I'm bothering you, you can put these on your ears and you won't have to listen to me, but you'll always know how much I love you.' Both girls were so pleased."

After all that preparation, it was gratifying to see all

the children welcome little Sara with open arms. Nobody appeared to feel displaced; in fact, little Colin felt so secure that he didn't seem to mind giving up his last born "birthright" to the new baby princess.

"Colin adores Sara and he helps me with her all the time," Diane commented. "The other day while he was holding her, he told me, 'Sara is the greatest thing that ever happened to our family.' I can't believe how everything has worked out so well, particularly after those first eighteen months when there were times when I thought we were crazy to try to put a marriage and our families together."

Their Blended Family Portrait Said It All

The more Diane and Alex talked, the more I was reminded of several Loving Discipline principles, such as relationships coming before rules, the whole being more important than the parts, and parents being in healthy authority over their kids.

"What about values?" I asked. "If you had to name the really important things that you live by in your home, what would they be?"

"Just being family and having a strong faith in God," Diane said quickly. "Alex and I both had church backgrounds, and we didn't want to lose the spiritual aspect of our lives. We found a church that we both liked, and we have taken the children ever since. Prayer is important to us."

One example of "being family" smiled down at me from the mantel. It was a family portrait, and I noticed that everyone was holding hands or had arms around someone else. Of course, little Sara was on Mom's lap, smack in the middle of one big circle of love.

When I commented on the photo, Alex said, "It's something we plan to do every year or so. We get lots of prints made and have them everywhere—all over the house, in wallets, on the refrigerator, even the dashboard of the car. It helps us all remember that we are a blended family and no longer two rended families."

"Obviously, you must have been listening a little bit at my seminar," I said. "What I hear you saying in your own words are the same things that I've been teaching for years about Loving Discipline—having a system that gives a family stability and puts the parents in healthy authority where there is plenty of love, but there are also limits."

"We've been to two of your seminars and have read several of your books," Alex offered. "As you can tell, we are big on traditional values, particularly mutual respect for each other. When Diane and I got married, we could see that there was friction between the girls especially, but we told everybody, 'Hey, you don't have to love each other—you don't even have to like each other—but we're all going to respect each other.' That's been a cornerstone of our family system."

This Is Not a Hotel, It's a Home

It didn't surprise me that Diane and Alex were firm believers in family meetings where everyone had a right to be heard, and it was okay to share feelings, including anger. During those meetings, they had worked out some rules together with the kids, including:

1. *Don't make decisions that affect other people in the family without checking with them first.* That's a

big one for Alex and Diane to remember because their kids are getting older and have schedules and commitments of their own.

2. *Don't touch other people's personal belongings without their permission.* This is a biggie for everyone, especially for Samantha, the only child.

3. *Everyone's individuality is important.* In our family, it's okay to be different from others. Colin likes this one because he's a typical last born who often shows up with his underwear hanging out of his back pocket.

4. *Each family member must pull his or her fair share of the load.* Colleen, the bossy firstborn, is very vocal about this.

5. *This is not a hotel, it's a home.* No one has license to come and go as he or she wishes. With a budding teenager and another one not far behind, this rule will get tested in coming years. Diane and Alex know that things have been going smoothly, but when the hormones come in, they plan to be ready.

"Something we try to model for the kids is respect for each other's needs," Alex told me. "We've tried to explain to the kids that we value democratic rule and that they can have a lot of input as to what our family does and how it operates. But bottom line, Diane and I are in charge, and sometimes we have to call the shots the way we see them. So far it's worked out well."

"We've All Grown to Really Love Each Other"

After interviewing Diane and Alex, I knew it would be hard to find a couple more creative or inspiring in its approach to a blended family. If there were a "Best Blended Family of the Year" award, they would have to be right there as top contenders. But as I was finishing up the manuscript for this book, I ran onto one more serendipity—an unexpected blended family pleasure that turned up when I really needed it.

I was doing an all-day seminar in a small town somewhere near the middle of nowhere, southeast of Tucson. Toward the end of the afternoon, I mentioned that I was working on a book dealing with blended families. Just before the final session, we took a fifteen-minute break and a young woman who looked to be in her late twenties approached me hesitantly.

She was short and had a few too many pounds, and while neat and clean, her clothes and hairdo were not really something out of *Vogue*. I suppose I was guilty of stereotyping again, but she had the look of someone who knew what being a mom was all about, even at her rather young age.

It turned out I was right. She introduced herself and got right to the point: "We're in a blended family. We have five kids, two of his, two of mine, and one of ours."

Her two were ages ten and six and that meant that she'd been married as a teenager, divorced, and remarried, all before age thirty. Her husband's two were twelve and eight, and they have a two-year-old together.

She mentioned that she had an eleventh grade education, and when she and her husband had remarried, they had both attended a class to learn parenting skills at a local community college.

"I'm sure you'll be interested in the textbook we used," she said with a smile. "It was *Making Children Mind Without Losing Yours*. When I heard you were going to be doing this seminar, I knew I couldn't stay away. My husband wanted to come, too, but he had to work today. I got up at five o'clock this morning and drove 120 miles to get here in time. I just wanted you to know that it's been hard, but we've made it."

Always on the alert for some good input, I said, "If you'd be willing, I'd love to have you tell me what advice you'd give to somebody who's trying to blend a family."

She smiled again, and her five-foot-three-inches seemed to grow taller before my eyes as she said with authority, "Number one, you and your mate have to stand together. If you don't stand together, you don't make it."

That sounds familiar, I thought to myself.

"Second, don't push the kids . . . never force them to love each other. I've made it a point to tell my husband's children and my own that they didn't have to love each other, but they did have to treat each other as well as they would treat the neighbors."

That sounds awfully familiar, too, I mused. *Has this woman somehow managed to gain access to my computer?* She went on: "And another thing that we've been strong on is telling the kids they have to solve their own problems. We always insist that they work things out among themselves. We won't settle their fights for them."

This is too much, I reflected, *she not only read* Making Children Mind, *she's using it!*

"You've made my day," I chuckled. "I'm impressed with your common sense and wisdom. I've been talking to a lot of stepfamilies, but I've never heard better advice put so succinctly. You have your own Ph.D. in 'Blended Family.'"

At that moment I thought it would be nice for this lady to meet Diane and Alex, whom I'd interviewed several months before. They would have a lot to talk about. And then my new friend added, "Oh, yes, one thing I also wanted to tell you is that we've all grown to really love each other."

I could see that in her eyes. It was that same look I had seen on the faces of Diane and Alex, something that made you know there was a connection—a blend of spirits. I told this mother that I was honored that she'd come all that way for my seminar. She apologized for not being able to stay for the final session—she had to get back home to get to her part-time job.

"I just wanted to say thank you for all the help you've been to our family," she said as we parted. I thanked her as well. She had been more help to me than she would ever know.

Later, as I drove into a blazing Arizona sunset, I thought about the blended family mother of five and hoped she'd made it back safely in time for work. I wondered about the home where she and her husband and children lived. Judging by the way she was dressed, they didn't have a lot of money. It was doubtful they had enough bedrooms for five kids and themselves. Perhaps they were trying to scrape money together to buy a bigger house—I didn't know.

In the eyes of many people, this family would probably be labeled as "not having much," but in the ways that count, they actually had it all. They had rules in their family, but they understood that relationships came first. Oh, they had their struggles, arguments, and problems, I was sure, but what had she said? *It had been hard but they had made it.* And then there were those special words, spoken with such a glowing smile: *We've all grown to really love each other.*

I stopped at a stop sign, then turned onto I-10 toward Tucson. Suddenly I realized I was tired. It had been another long bicoastal week, flying here and there and then back home just in time for my Saturday seminar.

I hadn't really been full of much energy when I'd come that morning, but now, somehow, I felt rejuvenated and encouraged. That little lady had given me new hope and resolve to keep getting out the message: Natural families, blended families—*any* family—can make it if they focus on what's really important.

We've all grown to really love each other.

Those words kept coming back, reminding me of a biblical passage known to millions, which talks about faith, hope, and love, and the greatest of these being love. And wasn't there something in there about love never failing?

I thought of the many families I knew who had everything—education, position, and practically every book on parenting ever written. And yet many of these families—some natural, some blended—had failed, even though the parents had worked so hard to make sure that their children would "have everything they didn't have when they were kids."

And that's the problem. People get so busy with their schedules and agendas, living in the fax-lane of life. They have no time to spend with their children, so they try to placate them with things. But kids really don't need all those things that their parents didn't have. They need loving discipline. They need to know that somebody really cares.

The sun was going down now behind distant mountains and there was just a red glow left in the sky. As the last rays of daylight failed, it struck me that many things fail. Cars, appliances, and gadgets wear out. Plans, strategies, and tactics backfire; formulas and carefully designed systems don't always work perfectly—including mine! But a blended family doesn't have to fail, and it won't, as long as Mom and Dad keep the goal in sight: that day when they can say, *We've all grown to really love each other.*

NOTES

1. Ray A. Kroc, *Grinding It Out* (New York: Berkley, 1978), 201. Quoted in Denis Waitley, *Seeds of Greatness* (Old Tappan, NJ: Fleming H. Revell Co., 1983), 198.

2. For more on the positive pleaser, see Kevin Leman, *Women Who Try Too Hard: Breaking the Pleaser Habits* (Fleming H. Revell Co., 1998).

3. Harold Bloomfield, *Making Peace in Your Stepfamily* (New York: Hyperion, 1993), 43.

APPENDIX
Recommended Reading

Dr. Bob Barnes, *Winning the Heart of Your Stepchild* (Zondervan Publishing House, 1997). A hands-on guidebook for men and women who face the special challenge of blending families. This book shows how to create an open atmosphere in your home, give reassuring answers to a child's questions, become a strong team with your new spouse, and deal with the inevitable challenges to a new authority figure.

Gary Chapman, *The Five Love Languages* (Northfield Publishing, 1992). According to Chapman, each person expresses and receives love through one of five different communication styles. This book will help you understand the five love languages and learn how to speak the language that your spouse will respond to best.

Gary D. Chapman and Ross Campbell, *The Five Love Languages of Children* (Northfield Publishing, 1997). This book helps you discover your child's primary love language and what you can do to convey unconditional feelings of respect, affection, and commitment that will resonate in your child's emotions and behavior.

Gary D. Chapman, *The Five Love Languages of Teenagers* (Northfield Publishing, 2000). Practical guidance on how to discover and express love in the language your teenager understands best.

Dick Dunn, *Willing to Try Again* (Valley Forge: Judson Press, 1993). Written by a pastor with thirty years' experience in ministry and step-family situations. Helpful for people preparing for marriage or those who are already "in the blender."

Kevin Leman, *The Birth Order Connection: Finding and Keeping the Love of Your Life* (Fleming H. Revell Co., 2001). Learn how birth order impacts your personal relationships and how you can find and keep a perfect complementary mate.

Kevin Leman, *Making Children Mind Without Losing Yours* (2nd edition, Fleming H. Revell Co., 2000). A compassionate and no-nonsense approach to child raising that teaches parents how to reasonably command discipline from their children while cultivating their love and respect.

Kevin Leman, *Making Sense of the Men in Your Life* (Thomas Nelson, 2001). A woman's guide to men—how they think and why they behave the way they do.

Kevin Leman, *The New Birth Order Book* (Fleming H. Revell Co., 1998). Your birth order powerfully influences who you are, who you marry, the job you choose, and the kinds of parents you are. Completely rewritten and expanded, this classic can help you understand yourself and how to get along better with others.

Kevin Leman, *What a Difference a Daddy Makes* (Thomas Nelson, 2001). Fathers set up their daughters for success, whether or not they live in the same house as their daughter. This book examines the special father–daughter relationship and tells dads how they can help their daughters grow into confident, loving adults.

Jane Nelsen, Cheryl Erwin, and H. Stephen Glenn, *Positive Discipline for Your Stepfamily: Nurturing Harmony, Respect, and Joy in Your New Family* (Prima Communications, Inc., 2000). "The essence of this book is a respectful approach to stepfamily discipline," says Margorie Engel, president, Stepfamily Association of America. "The scenarios are grittily realistic, and the wealth of positive suggestions ring true . . . this book is useful for both seasoned and novice parents and stepparents."

Video Series

Bringing Peace and Harmony to the Blended Family. A six-part series produced by Sampson Ministry Resources, (800) 371-5248.

Web Sites

Stepfamily Association of America: www.stepfam.org

The Stepfamily Connection: www.tsconnection.org

The Stepfamily Foundation: www.stepfamily.org